SISTAHFAITH

SISTAHFAITH

Real Stories of Pain, Truth, and Triumph

Marilynn Griffith

 HOWARD BOOKS
A DIVISION OF SIMON & SCHUSTER, INC.
New York • Nashville • London • Toronto • Sydney

Published by Howard Books, a division of Simon & Schuster, Inc.
1230 Avenue of the Americas, New York, NY 10020
www.howardpublishing.com

SistahFaith © 2010 by Marilynn Griffith

Library of Congress Cataloging-in-Publication Data

Sistahfaith : real stories of pain, truth, and triumph / compiled by Marilynn Griffith
    p. cm.
1. Abused women—Prayers and devotions. 2. Christian women—Prayers and devotions. 3. African American women—Prayers and devotions. I. Griffith, Marilynn.
  BV4596.A2S57 2010
  242'.4—dc22

                                                    2009039530

ISBN 978-1-4391-5277-5
ISBN 978-1-4391-7072-4 (ebook)

10 9 8 7 6 5 4 3 2 1

HOWARD and colophon are registered trademarks of Simon & Schuster, Inc.

Manufactured in the United States of America

For information regarding special discounts for bulk purchases, please contact Simon & Schuster Special Sales at 1-866-506-1949 or business@simonandschuster.com.

The Simon & Schuster Speakers Bureau can bring authors to your live event. For more information or to book an event, contact the Simon & Schuster Speakers Bureau at 1-866-248-3049 or visit our website at www.simonspeakers.com.

Edited by Lisa Bergren
Cover design by John M. Lucus
Interior design by Stephanie D. Walker

James Weldon Johnson, ed. "Turn Me to My Yellow Leaves," *The Book of American Negro Poetry.* New York: Harcourt, Brace and Company, 1922.
Scripture quotations marked NIV are taken from the *Holy Bible, New International Version*®. Copyright © 1973, 1978, 1984 by International Bible Society. Used by permission of Zondervan. All rights reserved. Scripture quotations marked KJV are taken from the *Holy Bible, Authorized King James Version.* Scripture quotations marked NASB are taken from the *New American Standard Bible*®. Copyright © 1960, 1962, 1963, 1968, 1971, 1972, 1973, 1975, 1977, 1995 by The Lockman Foundation. Used by permission. www.lockman.org. Scripture quotations marked NKJV are taken from the *New King James Version*®. Copyright © 1982 by Thomas Nelson, Inc. Used by permission. All rights reserved.

For Moriah, who dreamed with me of sisterhood.
I couldn't have done it without you, Doc.
I know you're shining, wherever you are.

CONTENTS

ACKNOWLEDGMENTS xi

INTRODUCTION: *In Search of Sistahood*,
by Marilynn Griffith..xiii
Serving Notice, a poem by Rosalyn Webb xvi
Selecting Your Sistahs xvii

CHAPTER ONE: *Tamar, a Sistah Ashamed*.................. 1
Winter Is Past, by Carlean Smith.................................. 3
The Kept One, by Bunny DeBarge.............................. 6
A Hateful Love, by Marilynn Griffith 8
Tamar's Triumph, a poem by Rosalyn Webb...................... 10
Twelve Weeks of Truth—Week One............................ 11

CHAPTER TWO: *A Sistahood of Scars* 12
Treasure in the Scars, by Sharon Ewell Foster..................... 13
Girl of Grace . . . Woman of Peace, a poem by
Tanya Bates 20
My Past Cannot Have My Future Blessings,
by Kisha Woods 22
Twelve Weeks of Truth—Week Two 29

CHAPTER THREE: *Tamar's Shame*............................. 30
My Own Creation, by Sonya Visor 32
Hush-Hush Stuff, by Little Sally Walker 35
Let Me Laugh, a poem by Wanda J. Burnside...................... 39
Twelve Weeks of Truth—Week Three 40

CHAPTER FOUR: *The Forgiving Hour*.......................... 41
Divinely Made, a poem by Wanda J. Burnside 42

Drowning Must Be a Terrible Way to Die,
    by Dr. Naima Johnston 43
Get Wisdom, Get Understanding, by Lady Catherine........... 51
I Loved a Boy, by Claudia Mair Burney 53
Twelve Weeks of Truth—Week Four 59

CHAPTER FIVE: *Tamar's Flight* 60
A Woman's Worth, by Delores M. Jones 61
Going Home, by Dorien Hage.. 65
How Dare You, by Robin Caldwell.................................. 69
Twelve Weeks of Truth—Week Five 76

CHAPTER SIX: *The Healing Pen*........................... 77
Life's Reintroduction, a poem by Carmita McWebb............. 78
Confession Is Good for the Soul, by Stanice Anderson 80
A High Price to Pay, LaVonn Neil................................. 89
Beyond the Scars, by Sharon Ewell Foster....................... 97
A New Name, by Marilynn Griffith 105
Twelve Weeks of Truth—Week Six 107

CHAPTER SEVEN: *My Sistah's Keeper* 108
Far Above Rubies, by Marilynn Griffith 109
A Place Prepared, by Marilynn Griffith.......................... 116
The Naked Pregnant Lady in the Yard,
    by Claudia Mair Burney 118
Twelve Weeks of Truth—Week Seven 121

CHAPTER EIGHT: *Her Robe, Royal No More*................. 122
Scars, by Claudia Mair Burney...................................... 123
Perfection, by Dr. Gail M. Hayes 125
When I Think I'm Unlovable, by Robin R. Wise 128
Uncovering Love, by Delores M. Jones............................ 133
Deliverance, a poem by Shelette Carlisle 136
Twelve Weeks of Truth—Week Eight 137

Contents

CHAPTER NINE: *My Rearguard* 139

    The Short Trip Back to Sanctuary, by Davidae Stewart 142

    Tamar's Wings, a poem by Marilynn Griffith 145

    Twelve Weeks of Truth—Week Nine 147

CHAPTER TEN: *Choose Life* 148

    Tea and Crackers, by Dr. Gail M. Hayes 149

    No Choice, by Marilynn Griffith 154

    Amazed by Grace, by Stanice Anderson 155

    Evergreen, by Marilynn Griffith 161

    Twelve Weeks of Truth—Week Ten 164

CHAPTER ELEVEN: *Garments of Praise* 165

    If I Were Her, by Claudia Mair Burney 166

    Two Minutes, by Dr. Gail M. Hayes 169

    My Heart Waketh, by Marilynn Griffith 173

    From Shame to Praise, by Dee East 176

    What If . . . I Had Never Been Sexually Abused?
        by Stephanie L. Jones 180

    The Day of Salvation, by Marilynn Griffith 184

    Twelve Weeks of Truth—Week Eleven 186

CHAPTER TWELVE: *A Healing Season* 187

    Raising the Roof, by Marilynn Griffith 188

    Brother, I'm Healed, a poem by Marilynn Griffith 190

    A Bare Witness, by Marilynn Griffith 192

    Healing Proclamation Prayers 195

    Twelve Weeks of Truth—Week Twelve 198

HEALING RESOURCES 199

ABOUT THE CONTRIBUTORS 201

ACKNOWLEDGMENTS

This book came through many hands and hearts. Thanks to Philis Boultinghouse, Lisa Bergren, Alysha Bullock, Karen Longino, and everyone at Howard Books/Simon & Schuster who read, edited, designed, or worked on this book in any capacity. You did an amazing job.

To the sistahs who trusted me enough to send me their stories, thank you for working, waiting, and praying!

To my agent, Wendy Lawton, thanks for believing in this book . . . and in me.

Fill, thanks for your love and patience, the preface to all my stories. You are a gift.

Donna McElrath, thanks for giving me life and for always sending a box full of something I need at the exact moment that I need it. How do you do that?

Ashlie, Michelle, Fill Jr., Ben, James, John, and Isaiah. Thank you for waiting through the years of late nights that became this book. I love you.

Mair, Sharon, and Stanice: Thanks for sticking with me. For real.

Joy, Carlotta, Melissa, Nancy, Claudia, Gail, Michelle, LeeShun, Katina, Barbara, Vickie, Lisa, Jackie, Viva, Sabrina, Venita, Jess, Vicki, Angela, Laura, Tammy, Kris, Kim, Linda, and all the women who have loved me and listened to me, thank you. Seriously.

Dr. Gail: You were there at the beginning, in the bone-fire. Thanks for the spark!

Robin Caldwell: You truly have an Andrew spirit. Thanks for making me push.

Glenda Howard: Thanks for your encouragement.

Tyora Moody: Thanks for your spirit, skill, and for seeing the vision when there was none.

Linda Dwinell, Carmita McCall, Rosalyn Webb, Melodie Kent, LeeShun Jackson, Mary Ardis, Barbara Joe Williams,

Katina Amoah, Shantae Charles, Annette Ponder, June, Michelle, Carlean Smith, and everyone I'm leaving out: Thanks for making the conference amazing. Rest up!

Dr. Harold Arnold Jr., Pastor Eliott Sheppard, Vincent Alexandria, and all the brothahs who "got" this book. Thanks for listening!

To my blog readers, newsletter subscribers, Twitter followers, Facebook friends, and members of the SistahFaith Network and all other places I sometimes disappear from. This is where I was. Forgive me?

To my pastor, Kent Nottingham, his wife, Debbie, and the Tallahassee Calvary Chapel family, thanks for teaching the Word and loving my family.

Jewell: I love you. I always have.

To my Jesus: You got me this time. I had no idea. Thank you.

IN SEARCH OF SISTAHOOD

Marilynn Griffith

Is there no balm in Gilead? Is there no physician there? Why then is there no healing for the wound of my people?

JEREMIAH 8:22 NIV

I always wanted a sister. My mother had four of them and although they had their differences, those old reel-to-reel movies of them dancing in my aunt's basement or the knowing smiles they shared across the table at holidays made me crave sisterhood. I sought it first in friends, not knowing really how to value myself, let alone other girls. Back then, people used me to suit their purposes and I used them to suit mine and we called it friendship, knowing that some things we said about other folks when they weren't around were said behind our backs too. Deep down, we knew that despite our best efforts, we were far from sisters, far from friends.

Still, I desired sisterhood, looking fondly at the sorority girls during college, enraptured by their secret dances and graceful calls. But that wasn't my road either. When I married a man with a sister, I thought I'd struck gold after sifting through roommates, coworkers, and girls down the street. I'd finally have a sister. But that wasn't to be either. She was already somebody's sister. She wasn't looking for another.

Around that time, I stopped seeking sisterhood and started seeking Jesus. It was a crooked path, like a never-ending treasure map, with God leaving gifts and drawing me to Him, step by step, verse by verse. He asked for everything I had: my daddy hunger, my need for sister love, the guilt, the shame, the confusion. Everything. And I gave it all, with one eyebrow raised, wondering what on earth He'd do with all of that. He was God, true enough, but that was a lot of mess. And I hadn't even had time to pack it up properly. Jesus took my stuff in trash bags and shoeboxes, old envelopes and yellowed notebooks. He took it all.

In the meantime, I wandered into churches, listening to people being referred to as "Sister So-and-so," only to have them look at me as though they wanted to run. Me, with my baby carrier and twisted slip, trying to get to Jesus. I wasn't "sister" material. Slowly, I realized you had to be a member of the church for over thirty years to break into the sisterhood. Well, I didn't have that kind of time. Still hoping, still hungering for a place to belong, for women to belong to, I moved on.

My journey took me on to other places, other crosses, other "sisters." This time, they had lace collars and flowered dresses, big hair and sunny smiles. And rules. Lots and lots of rules. But their tea tasted good and they seemed to have this Christian woman thing down to a science, so I stuck around, trying to learn all the rules. It was tough. After a while, I dug out my blue jeans and lipstick and crawled away. Nobody seemed to notice—and those who did notice didn't want to get in trouble—so with waving hankies and a few "We'll pray for you"s, I was on my way again.

Around this time though, a strange thing started to happen. Every now and then—often when I least expected it—God would send me what I know now was a sistah, a woman who clicked with me instantly, cared about me, and taught me something new about being friends, about being real. These women came from different backgrounds, but they accepted me into their circles, even when I didn't fully know how to take part.

When I retreated from them in silence because things were getting too close, they pursued me. When I chased them instead of Jesus so I wouldn't have to deal with my life, they corrected me. They taught me that sometimes the only way to heal a wounded woman is to break her anew and let things heal correctly, to pull off her scabs and clean out the infection, the pain.

Most of all, these women believed in God with me and for me, moving past the hedge of shame I'd placed around myself. Not only did they listen to me, they did something I didn't even know I needed.

They told me their stories.

They showed me their scars.

I learned then that every woman needs a safe place to bleed, a quiet place to scream, and friends to dress her wounds. I'd tried bleeding with others before, but those women left more infection than I'd started with. This time was different; there were still rules, but also relationships to go with them. This time I was heard. This time I got whole.

Sistah Who?

So who is a sistah? She's someone you can take your bra off with. Someone who can see you at your worst. Someone you don't have to explain things to because she's been there. She's someone who'll come to your aid even if she hasn't heard from you in ages. She's funny. She's serious. She's loud. She's quiet. She's peanut-butter brown. She's ebony-satin black. She's pecan tan. She's alabaster white. She loves people and loves God. She looks different on any given day, but when you meet her, you know her because she'll listen to your story . . . and tell you hers.

As I began to share my testimony across the country, something unexpected began to happen: I was sharing my friends' stories too. Everywhere I went, they went with me, either in person or in spirit. New sistahs came also, whispering their tales into the folds of my blouse, sending stories by e-mail, sometimes revealing things they'd never told anyone.

The women in this book have come a long way to meet you. Some of them write under a new name to protect their families. Others speak in their own name to save their lives. They've become broken bread and poured out wine and uncovered themselves to be your covering. There is a Bible sistah here too: Tamar, whose life was torn by the hands of her brother. As you read these stories, be comforted if you are afflicted (or afflicted if you are comfortable). Be clothed with the robe of many colors, the garments of praise. Walk with us on a journey past hurt, past shame, past rejection. A journey straight to the heart of God.

Serving Notice

Rosalyn Webb

I see you, I feel you
And at times think that my arms are too short
To reach out to you
But I've been where you've been
I've cried those same tears
Felt those same fears
And I made it through
And just in case we never meet
And you pass by my words on the street
Let them embrace you
Because I wrote this
To let you know that you're noticed.

Reprinted by permission from *To Whom It May Concern,* © 2006.

Selecting Your Sistahs

For some of you, reading this book will be a journey you'll take with God alone, but we'd love you to bring some sistahs along for the ride. The key is figuring out who those women really are. If you're already in a book club or Bible study, we recommend breaking into smaller groups for safe sharing. If you'll be traveling with friends, dig into the exercises below before you light a fire and start telling your tales . . .

1. Read Genesis 2:25. Did God create us to live in shame? Explain.

2. Read Psalm 89:45. Did anything happen in your childhood that made you grow up too soon? Do you have safe friends to discuss these experiences with?

3. Read Psalm 34:5. Name up to ten women in your life who keep you looking to the Lord and want to see you shine. If you can't name any (or enough), where might you discover these women?

4. Select three women from your list of ten above and as you work through the next section of the book, pray about becoming sistahs with them. Let them know about the book and ask them to pray about working through it with you.

5. As for how to go through the book, we recommend you call the study "Twelve Weeks of Truth," one for each of the chapters. Meetings can include discussion, sharing, using writing to heal or simply discussing the stories from the chapter. Which suggestions appeal to you? What are you most looking to get out of this book?

Seven Things to Consider When Forming Your SistahFaith Circle

1. *Bleed Where It's Clean.* Is this place, this person, a safe place to bleed? Will they point me back to Jesus when I'm done or infect me with their own bitterness?

2. *Don't Bleed to Be Seen.* Am I trying to be seen or calling others to be clean? If God calls you to share, it will never be just about you. Don't tell your testimony to get attention, but rather to release God's healing power.

3. *Stay Safe!* The Bible says to be wise as a serpent and gentle as a dove. If your abuser could still harm you and your family in some way, don't give all the details.

4. *Take It Slow.* Healing takes time. Don't try to be spiritual and skip the steps. There is a time to mourn and a time to dance, a time to mend and a time to heal. Take that time and let God lead you to the right places and people to share your testimony with.

5. *Lighten Up!* Yes, it's hard to imagine that an abuse story could be humorous or artistic, but it can. If you sing, write poetry, dance, do art . . . use your gifts to tell your story. If you're a funny person, don't make light of things, but smile and be honest. Let your light shine!

6. *Learn to Listen.* Not everyone you share with will have a Tamar story. If these stories are outside your experience, use this time to learn to listen, to really hear the testimonies of the women in your life.

7. *Keep It Confidential.* While there will come a time when the women in your group will be sharing their testimonies with others, now may not yet be the time. You will hear things that will both amaze you and sadden you, and one reaction will be to share the story with others. Wait until your

sistahs are strong enough to speak up with their own voices before you share their stories.

Prayer of Proclamation

Father God, I reject the lies the world has told me about myself. I accept the forgiveness, healing, and friendship only You can offer. Though I'm going to be reaching out to my sistahs, I reach up to You also, crying out with a loud voice. Hear me, O God. Draw me close to You. Bring me safe women, holy women, to hold me and hear me. Help me do and be the same for them. In Jesus's name, amen.

SistahFaith

CHAPTER ONE

TAMAR, A SISTAH ASHAMED

"But she answered him, 'No, my brother, do not force me,
for no such thing should be done in Israel.
Do not do this disgraceful thing!'"

2 SAMUEL 13:2 NKJV

As we hear the testimonies of the women in this book, we'll be hearing the echoes of another woman's story as well. A story from the Bible. In 2 Samuel 13, there is a story of a rich, famous man with many beautiful, broken children. One of his sons, Amnon loved his half-sister Tamar.

He loved her so much that he made himself sick, though he knew she was a virgin and out of reach. (The fact that she was his half-sister didn't seem to bother him, but I digress.) At least he cared about something . . . at first, anyway. Then he made the mistake of telling his cousin Jonadab, who the Bible describes as a "crafty man" (probably a "playa" in today's terms). Cousin J had a plan: Amnon would lie down and pretend to be sick and request Tamar to tend him. Dear old Dad would send little sis to take care of him.

Tamar came right away, hooking up some food and presenting it with a smile. Amnon didn't take the food. He was hungry for something else. He ordered everyone out of the room. (I have no idea why none of these people in the room couldn't have fed the old boy, but let's move on.)

He told Tamar to bring the food into the bedroom. (Hmm . . . he was already lying down. What's in there, ketchup?) I wonder if her smile faltered by this point, if she was starting to wonder . . . Still it was her brother, and her *sick* brother at that, so she followed him into the bedroom.

And he took hold of her, the Bible says. I'm not sure how, but it sounds pretty convincing. He told her to come and lie with him.

Despite her pleading (she even told him to ask the king for her hand instead of defiling her), Amnon used his strength to force her and lay with her. This action changed both of their lives forever. Amnon died because of it and Tamar remained in her brother's house, shut away from her father.

For some of the women in this book, there was a similar moment in their lives, a time when they were violated and covered in shame . . . a shame that only Jesus Christ can take away.

Winter Is Past

by Carlean Smith

My beloved spake, and said unto me,
Rise up, my love, my fair one, and come away.
For, lo, the winter is past, the rain is over and gone . . .

Song of Solomon 2:10–11 KJV

The Michigan winter held a cold chill that cut through my wool hat and gloves. It was nothing compared to the coldness I saw in his eyes. I curled my fingers into a fist to protect my hands, but I couldn't protect the rest of me.

My body shook, partly from the cold, but mostly from fear. In the split second since my best friend of fourteen (of our seventeen) years had gotten out of the car, her cousin had gone from good-natured big brother to cold-eyed captor.

"Where are you taking me?" I asked in a small, shaky voice. I looked out the window behind me, watching as my home and place of safety disappeared. I just wanted to go home.

He drove on, in the opposite direction. "Shut up before I throw you out the car," he said.

I looked for some kind of sign that this was the same person who had brought me and my friend a four-pack of wine coolers. He had ignored us while we sipped and laughed about things that only a seventeen-year-old would think were funny.

Now he was menacing and mean. I was afraid to speak for fear of offending him. We rode in silence down the highway. I curled my body in, my shoulders stooped. I was so scared. What was he going to do to me?

When we got back to his apartment, I was no longer his little cousin's friend. I was his victim. He came around to my side of the car and grabbed my right arm, daring me to try to run. I looked, in vain, for another soul outside. There was no one out with a blizzard threatening to let loose. *What's going to happen to me? I wondered.*

Inside his apartment, there was the musty odor of rotting wood, water damage, and old fried food. Clothes were piled on the floor and furniture. The pale green paint was dirt stained and peeling. We'd reached the place where I'd be robbed of my trust in people, my sense of safety, and my self-worth. This was the place where I'd start to hate myself, though I didn't know it then.

He released my arm and grabbed my neck, threatening again. "If you don't want to die tonight, you better take off your clothes and lay down."

I replied in a tiny voice, "Please, don't do this to me."

He looked at me with that same cold stare and pushed me on the mattress and box spring stacked on the floor.

When I got up later, I was a shell of my former self. I was tainted, ruined, and filled with shame.

In my mind, I belittled myself. I'd been too scared to protect my own virtue, too weak to protect my own body. He took me against my wishes and I couldn't stop him. So much was stolen from me that night. I didn't have the courage to fight and die for my honor. All I did was cry. All I had were tears.

He looked at me and said, "You were stiff. If you would've participated I probably would have fallen in love with you. Look at you, you're a mess. Fix yourself up so I can take you home."

I thought that meant I was no longer worthy of love, that no man would ever want me. Not even my rapist wanted me. I was full of hate and unable to forgive myself. I believed it was my fault, that I had somehow caused my assault. I believed I didn't deserve love.

He took me home in silence. My spirit was broken; my sense of right and wrong was distorted. I reached home, but the carefree girl was left behind on a smelly mattress. I lay on the steps, too weak to make it upstairs. I cried until my mother called my name. I answered her in what I hoped was a normal voice.

"Is that you? Are you okay?" she asked.

"Yeah," I lied, and ran to the bathroom. Nausea attacked me

with a force as violent as the earlier assault. I made it to the toilet bowl just in time. But I still felt sick, full of secrets I couldn't tell, for fear that everyone would blame me for letting it happen.

I wish I could say that I found healing and wholeness soon afterward. I didn't. I spent many years with intimacy problems and being sexually promiscuous. I started to live what I'd mistakenly believed about myself. I dulled the pain with drugs and alcohol. Unworthiness, fear, and self-hatred were my constant companions. I was my own worst enemy and greatest foe.

Then one day I met a man named Jesus who thought I was beautiful. Healing and forgiveness came. Healing for my spirit, that was broken at seventeen years old, and forgiveness for the man who in his own spiritual poverty took me against my will. Forgiveness for me, for not knowing how to protect myself, even though I probably couldn't have anyway.

These days I'm surrounded by love. My constant companions are the Father, Son, and Holy Spirit. My life is peaceful and full of joy. The days of the gray skies are far behind me. My shame has been washed away by the blood of the Lamb. I no longer hide behind a cloak of secrets and fear. I wake each morning to new mercies and more love than I knew was possible. Yet I say a prayer for all the hurting women who haven't found the healing, sweet love and peace that lie beyond the shame.

Father God, we thank You that winter is past. We praise You for calling us out of the rain and storms. Help us to be redeemed but also real women in this hurting world. In Jesus's name, amen.

The Kept One

Bunny DeBarge

The LORD bless thee, and keep thee:
The LORD make his face shine upon thee, and be gracious unto thee:
The LORD lift up his countenance upon thee, and give thee peace.

NUMBERS 6:24–26 KJV

I was fifteen years old when I started using drugs, so I needed to go back to that age to find myself emotionally and grow up. I needed to go back and remember things I had covered up with drugs. I needed to seek healing. The little girl in me who called for her mommy needed healing. My mama needed healing too, only I could not heal her and neither could she heal me; only God could do that. Mama did only what she knew how to do and that was to put it in God's hands and leave it there.

Well, I believe everything is done in seasons and I believe God knows the right season to do it in. He is always in control; we are the only ones who get out of control. He had a plan for my life before I was born. I may have gotten out of it but that does not mean that He stopped the plan. Satan also had a plan for my life. He peeked into the book that God wrote for my life. He saw my destiny and it was in his plan to stop me from making it.

Yes, there was so much that I had not faced and God had it in his plan just how and when to do it. As I am looking back on it, I was never alone, no matter how much I felt I was. He was there then and He is here today to take me through. The key word is "through." I had many things I needed to deal with: how it felt growing up being a mixed child and the mental and physical abuses we bore from a family member.

I needed to deal with the fact of being sexually molested by that family member and keeping it a secret for years. I needed to deal with my parents' denial of the sexual abuse ever happening. I needed to deal with living with that denial and how it affected my life, how it caused me to go to drugs in order to numb the pain from it.

I needed to deal with my life with my siblings during and after the abuse, with my life in the church world and most of all my relationship with my God, my life with Motown, my life as a star and my life as a fallen star.

My life was a mess and I needed to go back and find myself if I wanted to live out my destiny. All of these subjects that happened in my life were hidden and I was running from them all. I needed to cry a last cry. I had to go alone without anyone but God really understanding how I was doing it. I took Him with me this time, knowing He was always there anyway.

I was tired of pretending that things did not happen and everything was all right. I was tired of hiding secrets. I was tired of covering wrongs. I was tired of getting up only to fall again. I had to know why and I went to the Author of my book, my God, and I took him back with me and repeated each page of my book until I knew how to let go and what to let go of, when to let go and how to move on.

This is my season. I choose to start from this place in my life and go back in order to go forward. I choose to start here, at the beginning of my story, the story of God keeping a girl when no one else could.

Father God, thank You for keeping me, even when I didn't know what You were doing. May every woman reading this be blessed with wisdom, courage, and healing by the Holy Spirit. In Jesus's name, amen.

A Hateful Love

Marilynn Griffith

But she answered him, "No, my brother, do not violate me,
for such a thing is not done in Israel;
do not do this disgraceful thing!"

2 SAMUEL 13:12 NASB

When something is so broken, has always been broken, you begin to wonder when it cracked. Did it all fall off at once or were there little fissures, seams so small that they went unnoticed?

There was a major crack that day, that day when my heart splintered and we left home to go to Grandma's. Daddy didn't come. I never saw him again. Captain Kangaroo was there though. Faithful. Consistent. If someone had asked me then who was the best kind of man, I probably would have named the captain or Mr. Rogers. The most reliable guys in my life at the time weren't real.

Maybe someone should have told me that wasn't a good sign. Not that I'd have listened. Nothing could silence the man hunger in my belly, the abandonment in my bones. I learned soon enough that some men have a hunger too—a yearning. That yearning is bigger than a crack, worse than a splinter, something like a wrecking ball . . . something that orphaned my girlhood.

The first man, a teenager with an early mustache and full face, lay in wait, ready to swing that wrecking ball. Looking back, he seemed to know that tearing down my walls wouldn't take much time. He was just a guy from school, not one I paid attention to. When he knocked at the door, it didn't occur to me to ask how he knew where I lived. So smart, yet so stupid.

"Can I use the phone?" he asked. Needed to call his mother, had to get home. I wasn't allowed to have company, but wasn't this different? Someone was in need. If only I'd known what kind of need.

Almost blinded by the pain, I learned quickly about his needs. He smiled like men did on television before they proclaimed their love on soap operas. I did not smile back. I didn't love him. I really didn't know what love was beyond Maya Angelou's poems and my grandmother's cinnamon rolls. Laying there, saying no and not being heard, I decided love didn't exist.

Three hours later, my mother came home.

"Did you peel the potatoes?" she asked, ignorant of my demise.

"No."

She shook her head and gave me the "lazy" look. Another long day had worn her down.

I was tired too. Too tired, too humiliated, too afraid to explain. All I could do was stay on my feet, standing there broken, bleeding, and wondering why she didn't know, couldn't see. I somehow identified with the weariness in her voice, realizing not for the first time that she was fighting her own battles and had no eyes left to see mine. Though we did not touch and I did not tell, in that moment I understood her for the first time. I peeled the potatoes and cried myself to sleep.

Two weeks later, the boy came back and took our stereo. I guess my stolen goods didn't satisfy him. He never spoke to me again. He hated me more than he had loved me, if he had ever loved me at all. Ten years later, as a police officer defined rape to my bleeding friend, I choked back a scream.

That had happened to me, too.

Father God, thank You for Your faithful love. When shame comes knocking, please open the door and let it know that love lives here and there is no one home by that name. In Jesus's name, amen.

Tamar's Triumph

Rosalyn Webb

Her legend was left
upon the steps
as she wept.
We are Tamar's Triumph
Those who have walked down painful roads
Of life
And lived
Those who've been took
And still managed to give
Those who were blinded
And had vision restored
To peer into the reality of dreams
Those who defied labels of desolation
And healed to become the wealth of nations
Her legend was left
upon the steps
as she wept.

Reprinted by permission from *To Whom It May Concern*,
© 2006 Rosalyn Webb.

Twelve Weeks of Truth —Week One

"For where two or three come together in my name, there am I with them."

<small>MATTHEW 18:20 NIV</small>

Whether you've decided to work through this book on your own or among a group of sistahs, we applaud you. Digging deep into your past takes work, effort. As you move forward, know that you're already among a group of friends, seen or unseen. We're all in this together.

DISCUSSION QUESTIONS

1. Which of the stories in this chapter sparked the greatest response in you? What about it was memorable for you? If that woman had been your friend, how would you have helped her, heard her?

2. If you haven't already, read 2 Samuel 13 and discuss what happened to Tamar. Do you have a Tamar tale of your own? If you don't, how can you support the other sistahs in the group without letting it turn into a pity party?

3. One of the biggest problems people have with the church is hypocrisy. Your assignment this week is to begin writing your real testimony—and not the "Blessed Assurance" version either. Get a notebook and list three events (good or bad) that were turning points in your life. Choose from those and write for ten minutes about the event. Close your entry with a prayer for all involved, including yourself.

Father God, give us the endurance to make it to the end of this study. May we make lifelong friends here. In Jesus's name, amen.

CHAPTER TWO

A SISTAHOOD OF SCARS

But he was pierced for our transgressions,
he was crushed for our iniquities;
the punishment that brought us peace was upon him,
and by his wounds we are healed.

ISAIAH 53:5 NIV

Amnon wounded Tamar in many ways. She never recovered. We, the women of this book, have been wounded too, but we have also been healed, by the wounds of Jesus. In fact, without us showing our scars, no one would ever know that we'd been hurt. Sometimes we forget ourselves. We dance, sing, write, teach, love like there is only today and that's all there's even been.

But then one day, we see it, the corner of pain untucked and hanging from beneath someone's accomplishments. We acknowledge that while our silence hides our wounds, it also hides our healing. So instead of skirting the issues, we chose to show you, to share with you, our scars. Doing so isn't always as easy as one might think.

Treasure in the Scars

Sharon Ewell Foster

But we have this treasure in earthen vessels, that the excellency of the power may be of God, and not of us.

2 CORINTHIANS 4:7 KJV

In the summer of 1997, I sat at my desk in a temporary trailer at Fort Meade. What I felt—wearing my best dressed-for-success suit, my hair in a ponytail with a large bow—was peace. I had spent the previous year working at the Pentagon on a publication called the *Early Bird* and was enrolled in an executive leadership program for women. A long title and even longer money, along with an endless stream of clothes, high heels, and makeup, were all I told myself I wanted. All this success would be perfect because, like most people, I wanted to cover my scars.

In many cultures scars are beautiful—they denote honor and standing. Through intricate patterns, man-made scars share the story, the timeline, and the history of the one who bears them.

But I didn't grow up in one of those places. I was born in Texas and grew up in Illinois. In both those places scars are not considered a good thing. Growing up with four brothers, I always seemed to be falling down. My mother invested in a lot of cocoa butter, rubbing that chocolate-smelling fat on my wounds, hoping that her only daughter wouldn't be a scarred-up mess who would bring shame on the family. "Be careful now." Pain and worry made her frown. "You don't want to wear stockings and have scars showing through."

When I was a girl, sheer stockings were a right of passage. Stockings meant everybody could see your legs, it meant attention from boys, and it meant someday there would be a trip down the aisle. But no one wanted to see dark marks and raised, torn skin. I would have to be perfect for anyone to want me.

I wasn't perfect. I was scarred and I worked harder at covering it than at anything else in my life. My beautiful mother was scarred too. She covered her pain with silk stockings, powder, and lipstick. She covered her pain by not telling her story, a story so difficult *not* to tell that she avoided people. A story I tell you now:

In the sixteenth year of her life, my mother was raped. That rape resulted in pregnancy. As a result of her pregnancy, my grandfather banished her from the family home. My grandmother then left the love of her life to be with my mother. In that same year, my grandmother died from a stroke, leaving my mother alone with a newborn in a world that shunned unwed mothers. Shortly after my grandmother's death, baby Atlas also died, leaving my mother completely alone.

My mother did not tell her story. No one outside the family knows the story, maybe my brothers don't even know it—I didn't learn about it until I was in my thirties. Instead she covered her pain with false strength—*I'm not afraid of anything*—with her teaching position, successful husband, and perfect, beautiful children. My mother was a sensitive, creative woman, but her hidden wounds never healed. As much as she loved us, she was also angry, abusive, and manipulative. We lived with the specters of rejection and abandonment over our heads, never knowing what would stir her rage.

My career, like meth for a junkie, helped dull the pain. If I could just get more—more money and a more prestigious title—that would make everything better. The leadership program, with its many requirements, was part of my plan for getting more. One requirement was career exploration. That one would be easy. I already knew what I wanted: long money and long title. I knew about exploring careers; I didn't know about exploring me.

As usual, my answer to everything was money. My bill problems were the reason I was sad sometimes. A better position would also get me away from the angry, frustrated people who seemed to pop up everywhere in the workplace to make my life hell.

I only examined the truth when I had no other choice, like

when I got angry one day and slapped my beautiful, sweet five-year-old daughter on the back. Hard. I can still remember the image of my full handprint on her little back. For less than a moment, I started to justify to myself why it was okay—I had been hit, hadn't I? I turned out all right, didn't I? I needed to do it so she wouldn't grow up to be a bad person, didn't I?

Just as quickly, a childhood promise came back to me: When I grew up, if I grew up, I would treat my own children differently. I would remember that they were God's children, children temporarily entrusted to me. Right then, I faced the truth: Discipline doesn't mean abuse, and there were ways to discipline without harm. So I went far enough on the journey of self-discovery to save my daughter, but I didn't go far enough to save myself.

I put my energy into my career instead. Not that it helped. I wasn't rising quickly enough to suit my needs and people continued to pester me. I prayed. I tried to be a good person, I sang in the choir, I gave to the poor, and I did my job well. What was the problem? Why did happiness elude me?

Riding along one day, I heard an inspirational speaker, Joyce Meyer, talk about being molested by a family member and how it had impacted her life. It reinforced statements I had heard from people like Oprah Winfrey.

Comparative mythologist Joseph Campbell, author of *The Hero with a Thousand Faces,* would call Oprah and Joyce heralds: people who beckon the heroine to begin the journey. I didn't want to begin the journey. What did my being abused and not being the favorite kid have to do with how I was feeling? All that was behind me. Why stir around in that mess? All of us had moved on with our lives. I wasn't a child anymore. None of that old baggage controlled me. Besides, thinking about it was painful. It made me feel ashamed.

As I worked on assignments at the Veterans Administration and for the Joint Chiefs of Staff, I began to examine the territory of my own life. This journey of the heart took more courage than anything I'd ever done. I was wounded and no amount of gauze, no career, and not even any amount of makeup could truly mask the pain.

I uncovered the wounds one by one, starting with my mother, starting with a memory: When I was fifteen, on one occasion, I came home from school. Only my mother was home. She was in the kitchen putting the finishing touches on an elaborate meal. It had been a good day at school, the food smelled great, and I let my guard down enough to be happy. My mother told me to go to the table. *Star Trek* was playing on the television. She sat down. I looked up from my plate. She punched me in the face. Hard. She started crying and ran from the room. Holding my face and also crying, I went upstairs to my room trying to figure out what had happened.

When my father came home, he told me to apologize to my mother for upsetting her. What had I done? I still don't know. He told me, "You know she loves you. You are both just too much alike." It was a very strange way to love. I don't love that way.

Other family members had wounded me too. Used me. One of my best friends used to call it being the *n-word* in the family. When people were angry, disappointed, I was the cat they kicked. I was molested by some of my family members; when they had an itch, they used me to scratch it.

Instead of being protected, I was beaten for talking about what happened to me. "Evil May Jones," my mother called me. I didn't want to add being mean to the list of adjectives that described me, so I surrendered. I learned to hide. Perhaps if I was invisible, if I stayed out of the way, if I didn't try to be special, things would go better for me. But there was no way to stay out of the way.

My brothers were the special ones. They were the smart ones. Even though people outside of my family and school and at church told me I was special, within my family there were no special plans for my life. Though I was in the band, in the chorus, in the National Honor Society, and though I wrote for the school newspaper, my family did not talk about what I would become. No one expected me to go to the ball. "Make sure you can type," my mother told me. "You will always be able to get a job typing," she said, and I believe she meant the best for me.

Though my assignments in the leadership program were teaching me about the government, my journey was teaching me about myself. I realized that I'd been confused about what love really was, that I'd felt unlovable and unable to receive those who wanted the best for me. It left me afraid to have too big a dream for myself. Who did I think I was?

I also realized why mean, abusive people seemed to find me. Those were the people I knew and so I'd allowed them into my world. There were wonderful people around me also, but I gave more power and attention to the abusers.

Some of my wounds are from things I did to myself—looking to dull my own pain. Any kind of love was better than no love. My love was a boy who showered me with attention and compliments. He protected me, held me, and talked to me. I didn't know anything about life or love, let alone birth control. I got pregnant at sixteen. But I was forced to have an abortion, to hide the scar. It was just one more wound to hide.

All of the wounds debilitated me. I was shamed by my childhood molestation, which began before I even entered school. Both the shame and the abuse got worse as I got older. Then came the abortion—having to sneak out of town aboard flights with a password, having to return home and hide what happened, only made things worse. I was evil, worthless, and a harlot. If my own family didn't love me, how could God love me after what I'd done?

But there was help for me. The inspirational speaker, Joyce, was also what mythologist Campbell calls a mentor, a source of wisdom, during this step. I bought tape after tape after tape of hers. I read book after book after book, wandering through bookstores and libraries. I watched television shows about people who had recovered from abuse.

I cried through much of this step. I was angry. Each memory brought new tears and pain. But I was on the journey now, and I would finish what I had begun.

I had moved far away from my family, something I shared in common with many military members. But suddenly they were calling. I worried that if I confronted them, I would lose control. I was afraid I wouldn't be able to forgive. I was afraid I wouldn't be able to love.

I share with you now what I did not want to face then. I share it not to shame anyone or out of bitterness. I share it to give hope.

Around this same time, as part of my leadership training, I completed an inventory that helped me look at how I handled confrontation. The inventory told me that there were other response options, something between avoiding confrontation entirely and nuclear explosion. I resolved that I would begin to speak up.

I worried that taking this next step on my journey might cause me to lose what little family association I had left. Even if that association was negative, it was better than nothing. How could I survive without them? And like everyone else, I wanted to be a part of a whole, even if that whole was flawed.

Perhaps, I thought, if I demanded more of my family, they would rise to the occasion. If they didn't, then I wasn't losing much but heartache, and I might gain self-respect and peace.

My family of origin didn't like the new me. They wanted me to stay in my old place, quiet and complacent. Discussing our past felt like I was trying to hurt them. Of course, no one thought about how hurt I was.

They still don't invite me to frankfurter parties and marshmallow roasts. My father and brothers, even since I've become an author, have reminded me that no one wants to hear what I think and that I am not the savior of the world. One family member, whom I love, tried to have me arrested because I confronted him about the abuse, abuse that continued into another family.

Though my family of origin does not love me any more, I have more self-respect and more peace after examining my scars, understanding where they began and ended. I am more comfortable in my own skin. And as I began to stand up for myself, speaking to them with love and respect, I also began to find the courage to disregard the labels they had attached to me. I wasn't evil. I wasn't lazy. I wasn't unable to take care of myself.

I was a treasure.

Father God, we thank You for revealing the treasure inside us. Give us wisdom in how to share the goodness You've put inside us with people who will appreciate it. In Jesus's name, amen.

Girl of Grace ... Woman of Peace

Tanya Bates

I woke up this morning and looked in the mirror.

What I saw today was different than any other day.

Yesterday, I saw myself . . . a sinner, ugly, black, scarred, stained.

Before I went to bed, I said my prayers to the One who created it all.

I woke up this morning and looked in the mirror.

What I saw today was different than any other day.

Today, I saw myself . . . saved by grace, beautiful, black, washed clean, eyes filled with hope and peace.

What caused the change?

I finally decided that there was One who was greater than I was.

One who promised me that He would wash me white as snow.

My only responsibility was to proclaim Him, call Him by His name.

Believe like I have never believed, trust like I have never trusted.

I had to forgive, as I now understood that I was forgiven.

I had to love like I now understood that I was loved.

I had to extend mercy and grace, as I now understood that grace and mercy were mine.

What I see today is a girl of grace, kissed on the forehead by a Father who

Not only created me, but constructed me divinely for His purpose.

I see what I will be tomorrow, I see what I was in the past, and I see what I can be on this day.

I am a girl of grace fashioned in the image of the Creator, who makes me new each day.

Dear Creator, I accept my commission as a girl of grace, a daughter of yours. Destined for greatness.

Yes, I am a girl of grace. I now walk with my head high filled with the grace and mercy that was extended to me due to a beneficent and merciful Creator.

My Past Cannot Have My Future Blessings

Kisha Woods

Know also that wisdom is sweet to your soul;
if you find it, there is a future hope for you,
and your hope will not be cut off.

PROVERBS 24:14 NIV

"Kisha Woods, Dr. Raines will see you now," the nurse said.

As I walked down the hall I began to feel a bit embarrassed as to why I was here to see a psychiatrist. I always thought they were for the mentally disturbed, not for someone who can't get intimate with her man. I couldn't believe I'd let my best friend, Gail, talk me into coming to see a shrink. I thought I should just turn around and deal with my issues another way. As I turned around to head out the door, I bumped into a brown-skinned, petite woman wearing glasses.

"Excuse me," she said as she bent down to pick up the papers she'd dropped.

"Oh, I apologize, let me help you," I said as I bent down to help her pick up a chart.

"Hello, I'm Dr. Raines." She stuck her hand out to shake mine.

"Hi, I'm Kisha." I shook her hand while she gazed over at the chart I was holding—which was my own.

"Oh, you're my next patient. Sorry we had to meet in the hallway like this." While taking my chart out of my hand, she invited me into her office. As I stepped inside, I couldn't believe it. This room resembled something out of a designer's magazine. She instructed me to have a seat on the chaise lounge.

"What brings you in today, Ms. Woods?"

"A friend suggested that I come sit with you."

"What were you two talking about when she made the suggestion?" Dr. Raines asked.

"We were talking about my boyfriend."

"Is he abusive?"

"No, he's actually the perfect gentleman, and I'm afraid that I might lose him."

"Why do you feel this way, Ms. Woods?"

"I can't get intimate with him. I love James dearly, he's respectable, has morals, he's the perfect man for me—I just can't do it."

"How does James feel about this?"

"He drops little innuendos, but I always brush him off."

"Do you think he loves you?"

"Yes, I know he does. He proposed to me last week."

"What did you tell him?"

"I told him yes, but the next day I started feeling bad because I don't think marriage will change the way I feel about intimacy. As hard as I try, I just can't give him what he deserves."

"Are you attracted to him?"

"Yes."

"So I take it you and James have never been intimate?"

"No, we've come very close a few times, but I always stop him."

"Are you a virgin?"

"No."

"How old were you when you lost your virginity?"

"Fourteen."

"Do you still speak with the young fellow?"

"Well, it was actually my uncle."

"Did he rape you?"

"The first time, yes, but after that he convinced me that it was what girls my age were supposed to do until they found a boyfriend, and once I found a boyfriend, I'd be the woman he needed me to be."

"How old was your uncle?"

"He had to be about twenty-three or twenty-four."

"And he was having sex with you?"

"Yes."

"Did you ever tell anyone?"

"I was afraid until a few years ago; I told my ex-boyfriend, the father of my son, and my friend Gail."

"How many children do you have?"

"Two."

"How did you manage to have two kids, not being comfortable with sex?"

"Once I stayed away from my uncle I met another man—he's the father of my sixteen-year-old. I was still young and thinking I was doing what I was supposed to do because of what my uncle had told me. This other man was a good guy, but he died in a car accident after I had my daughter. Then I met a man, the father of my eight-year-old. That relationship was very abusive; he would force himself on me, and I ended up pregnant."

"Since you've been older, have you been in contact with this uncle?"

"Not really; one lives in Alabama, and the other one is in jail."

"The other one?"

"Yes, there were two of them."

"Why is the other one in jail?"

"For molesting my little cousin."

"Are these your mother's brothers or your father's?"

"My father's."

"Are your parents still together?"

"No."

"Are you and your family close?"

"My mom and I are close, but I'm not close with my dad and sister anymore."

"What happened?"

"It's a long story."

"Relax and take your time," she said, as she poured me a glass of lemonade.

"Well, my dad is financially blessed, and he helps us out a lot.

One day I needed three hundred dollars extra to make ends meet. I asked my dad and he gave me the normal 'You need to get it together' speech he would always give us whenever we would ask him for money. Well, a few months later, my children and I stayed at his house so I could do laundry, something me and my sister took turns doing.

"While I was in the laundry room, Dad said he needed to talk to me, so I went to his room and he started fussing about his money. I had just paid a deposit to move into my new place so I really didn't have it. When I told him that he said we'd have to work out something because his hours were cut and his money was low.

"I told him I'd pay him back when I got some money. He told me some things I could do in front of him that would make the debt even. Some things a woman never expects to hear from her father.

"I stood there in disbelief for about twenty seconds. I then asked, 'What did you just say?' He heard the seriousness in my tone so he started laughing and said, 'You know I'm just playing with you.' I felt completely violated—this was my biological father; how could he say something like that to me? I ran to the laundry room and took my wet clothes out of the washing machine, shoving everything into a laundry basket.

"I grabbed my kids and stormed out of the house, trying to hold back my tears, so the kids wouldn't start asking questions. When I got to my house, my boyfriend was there packing the rest of our things.

"I felt a sense of relief, thinking I had someone I could talk to. When I walked inside, he could tell something was wrong, so I told my daughter to take her little brother in the back room and watch TV. I went into the room and I cried out to my boyfriend. He pushed me back and said, 'I don't want to touch you after what you just told me.' I couldn't believe my ears; I'd been with this man for seven years. He started yelling at me about how I always went over there, and I knew how my uncles were, and the clothes I wear were too revealing. He then slapped me across my face so hard I fell to the floor, and my nose started bleeding. He came over to me and started kicking me. He forced himself on me while he continued beating me.

"I started to wonder if it was me that caused my so-called loved ones to act like this. He started screaming at me, telling me to call *him* Daddy. Those words would not dare come out of my mouth; I began to call on Jesus, saying, 'God, please help me.' From all the commotion that was going on, my daughter came to my door and said, 'Mommy, are you okay?' He yelled at her through the door and put his clothes on, got his big leather belt, and went out there and started beating her. I grabbed a dress, threw it on my bruised body, and went out to stop him. When he stopped hitting her, he started beating me with the belt. When he finally quit, he stormed out the house and got in his car and drove off. All I could do was hug my daughter and apologize for bringing him into our lives. I called the police and they came out and took pictures of our bruises. Then I called my sister and told her everything that happened and that I was never going over Dad's house again, and I was done with my boyfriend. She felt really bad and kept asking, 'What is wrong with our dad?'"

"What happened with your boyfriend?" Dr. Raines asked.

"The police arrested him, and the judge gave him a five-year sentence."

"There must be more to this story since you said you and your sister fell out as well."

"Yes, we did. A few months had passed; I got a house, me and my kids started going back to church, I got a new car and a good job. Things were really looking good for me. I thanked God daily and asked him to keep negative people away from me so I could continue to be blessed. From time to time, I would hang out with my sister and our friends that we grew up with. One night we went out but I was too tired to drive home, so I spent the night at my sister's. I heard her house phone ring early the next morning and could tell by the conversation something was wrong. She hung up and said, 'Kisha, come on, Daddy just got robbed at gunpoint.'

"I jumped up and threw on my clothes. I called James, who's actually my fiancé now and told him what had happened and as I was telling him, something came over me and I changed my mind about going. James knew what my dad had said to me, but he said, 'Go, Kish, your dad needs you. I'll meet you there.' When I got there, the police were leaving and my father was in good spirits considering he had just got robbed. For some reason I felt no sympathy for him. As he was telling us what happened, I said, 'I'm glad they didn't hurt you and you're alive, but I really don't care,' and I got in my car and left with my friend following in the car behind me.

"The next day my sister came over and I could tell something was bothering her. When I called her later to make sure everything was all right, she started accusing me of a nonchalant attitude about Dad's robbery."

"Did you try to talk to her?"

"Yes, I did. She is my baby sister and I pretty much raised her, but she went back and told our family and friends that I set him up. Everyone started acting funny toward me, whispering among themselves that I was scandalous. But no one knew why she thought that. It was very painful. The ones that were loyal to me were telling me to be careful because the people that were closest to me were envious and trying to assassinate my character. So I slowly started backing away. James and I became closer; he was there for me through it all, telling me it was God's intention to move negative people out of my life to make room for the positive ones."

"Have you talked to your dad or your sister lately?"

"Yes, but it's not the same. I don't feel comfortable around my dad, and I don't trust my sister."

"I suggest you get in contact with your uncles and tell them how you feel about what they did to you; tell your dad the same. Try to embrace your sister; she feels like she's losing you. Even though you have separated yourself from her, call her sometime to see how she's doing. Show her that regardless of all of the chaos she caused, you're still standing and you still love her. Try to not let your past come in contact with your future. Before you get married, I would suggest premarital counseling with your pastor.

"Not only am I a doctor, but I'm also a minister, and I believe it can be God taking you in the direction He wants you to go, so you can wait until you're married to become intimate. Does James go to church?"

"Yes, we go together."

"Great! Well, the two of you go to six weeks of premarital counseling and come back and see me in about twelve weeks. I just want to give you time to contact your uncles and your dad. You don't have to see them face-to-face; a letter with a return address, leaving room for a response, is always good, or maybe even a phone call would be nice."

"Okay, thanks, Dr. Raines, I'll see you in a few months."

"Take care, Ms. Woods."

The day James and I finished with premarital counseling, we decided to sneak off to city hall and get married. After the private ceremony, we had a very intimate honeymoon in Santa Barbara in a suite overlooking the water for two days. My sister and I are cool again, my dad apologized, and so did one of my uncles. I didn't hear from my uncle who's in jail. I guess you can say his situation speaks for itself.

By the time I saw Dr. Raines again, James and I were married and expecting a child. She was impressed, but I knew it was Christ who'd brought me through to these blessings. It was this that my past was trying to keep me from. I'm thankful it didn't succeed.

Father God, thank You that my past was not able to keep me from my future. Bless every family struggling to live in the present and looking forward to the future. Reveal to me the glorious destiny You have planned for my life. In Jesus's name, amen.

Twelve Weeks of Truth
—Week Two

A father to the fatherless, a defender of widows,
is God in his holy dwelling.

PSALM 68:5 NIV

We are all someone's daughter, we were all once some man's little girl. Our relationships with our fathers, bad or good, can shape our relationships with other men. It can even shape our relationship with God. Discuss the questions below with your group and complete the writing exercise.

DISCUSSION QUESTIONS

1. Take a few minutes each and share your best memory of your father with your sistahs. Do you think your relationship with your earthly father has affected your relationship with God? What is your relationship with your father today?

2. Tamar went to her half brother at her father's request. When things went bad, Tamar begged Amnon to go to their father and ask for her hand. He chose to shame Tamar instead. Why do think he did that? Did the stories in this chapter tell a similar or different tale?

3. Take the same notebook where you started your testimony and write down one good thing that your father gave you, either directly or genetically. As a group, pray the prayer below:

Father God, I thank You that I am no longer the walking wounded but the healed hopeful. Though earthly fathers may fail, You never fail. I accept my father for who he was and who he is, knowing that it is my Father in heaven who defines who I am. In Jesus's name, amen.

CHAPTER THREE

TAMAR'S SHAME

*Those who look to him are radiant;
their face are never covered with shame.*

PSALM 34:5 NIV

Shame is a powerful thing. A hurting thing. Especially when you haven't done anything wrong, when folks are supposed to love you, to cover you, and they don't. They can't.

It's the smear on the garments of virgins, the gall in the cup of Christ, the venom of the accuser. Shame is the voice that comes calling at midnight, questioning purpose, murdering passion. It's the voice that asks, "Has God truly said . . . ? To *you*? I mean, come on . . ." This thing, this shame, it doesn't even bother to hiss, but it dares to speak clearly. Articulately. Boldly.

It comes to us, baiting, waiting, wondering if we'll give in, if we've forgotten who we are in Christ now, who we were in the world then. We remember enough to know that we don't have time for these games. We have work to do, love to give.

On these nights, we're thankful that we serve a God who holds court at all hours. He stands ready at all times to proclaim us innocent. We come to Christ and collapse. No need to explain. This isn't the first time.

"There's someone here to see You," we say.

He moves toward us, this Brightness, this Christ. Though we can't see His face, the Light bends like a smile. Thunder cushions his feet. Lightning dances from his fingertips. "You have forgotten who you are."

We look up at our sustenance, our Life. Jesus is sweet to us now, too sweet for us to spare a breath for the accuser.

The Light explodes into a sea of stars, pinpricks of warmth that brush our skin, wash us. The Light of our darkness. The sea of my tears.

The Light speaks. "I knew about all of that, but I chose to

30

forget." Light shifts, spotlighting those who've come along. "You should forget too, daughters of light. Go forth, and do not be ashamed."

The verdict is music to our ears. "Not guilty."

Relief settles around our shoulders, now slack with joy. At our feet are films, thin like egg whites, strong as secrets.

Masks of shame.

If you're still holding on to yours, let it fall away. If you've trusted Christ for your salvation, you're someone new.

My Own Creation

Sonya Visor

Therefore, if anyone is in Christ, he is a new creation; the old has gone, the new has come!

2 CORINTHIANS 5:17 NIV

At nine years old, when most little girls are jumping rope, playing with dolls, or learning to braid hair, I endured molestation from trusted family members. They forced me to do things that a child should never experience. Family members, who were supposed to love and protect me, touched and fondled me. My sense of security fled because of another's wrongdoing. It created cracks in my foundation that altered my life forever. Fear and depression boomed in me. Trouble and shame pursued me, yet I felt special.

As I look back over my life, I realize that God kept me. How? You see, right before they tried to take what wasn't theirs, something happened to stop them. Either the phone rang or someone knocked on the door. My most vivid recollection is when my oldest sister called my name. She knew what was happening, but being in the same situation, she could do nothing. God always made sure that they didn't enter the innermost court. Let me make it plain; they never scored a home run. But believe me, all the other stuff they did was enough. This wasn't what pushed me close to the edge, but it taught me how to cover up or pretend that all is well. I became a perfectionist at wearing a mask.

I felt dirty and ashamed for their sin. Like so many, I wondered, *Why me?* God knows everything about us. He knows what each day holds; He could have prevented this chapter in my life. But it was all a part of the plan, *my* plan. Even though I was in the pathway of another's free will.

All of this drama created something in me that I didn't like. I started to notice in myself a very familiar spirit or behavior at certain times. I just dismissed it. I didn't know it then, but I know it now—what I went through had a hand in creating my character. On the outside I mirrored a happy child, but on the inside I was crying out for help. No one could see it though because I'd decided to live the way others thought I should. No one could see the true me anymore. I was operating out of what I had become—my own creation.

Imagine standing in the line at your local grocery store, bank, or McDonald's and making eye contact with the woman in front of you. Your eyes lock and you briefly look away. When you make eye contact again, this time she glances away. But there was something in her eye. Something that captured you, but you couldn't quite detect what was there. You don't think too much about it; you're just waiting your turn in line. The next day, you casually take a look at your daily newspaper and you see the woman.

There's a picture of the lady you saw in the line yesterday. The caption reads, *Woman found dead in bedroom.* You are speechless at this point because as you read further you find that the death wasn't a result of a burglary, an accident, or natural causes. No, this death was the result of her own hand. How could someone who was standing in line ordering Happy Meals come to the conclusion to just up and take her life?

That woman in the line was wearing a mask. She was simply going through the motions of life, doing what she knew to do, a routine, a familiar way of operating and getting through the day. What if she had told somebody? Maybe she had told somebody that she felt like giving up and they didn't listen. Maybe she was crying and nobody could hear. This lady was in a desperate place and now finally people were listening, but she was gone. She was boxed in by circumstances, scarred by other people's choices. People may have hurt this woman and there were probably things that she had done in her life that she wasn't proud of. But still what would make someone willingly leave his or her family or friends? What is so bad in life?

Whatever it was . . . I truly can say today that I understand. I was just like that woman in line until one day . . .

I took off my mask.

Father God, thank You for making us new and removing all our masks. Bless every woman reading with deliverance and healing. Give us relationships where we can be real. In Jesus's name, amen.

Hush-Hush Stuff

Little Sally Walker

*For there is nothing covered, that shall not be revealed;
neither hid, that shall not be known.*

LUKE 12:2 KJV

What a revival!

I love revivals. Always have. And of all the spirit-filled services I've witnessed, our church's summer revival ranks number one on my list. On this particular night, the guest evangelist blessed my heart with the assurance, "The battle is not yours . . . it's the Lord's."

And not a minute too soon. With all the dissension festering at home, I yearned for a power-packed word from God.

Driving home from church, I continued singing and praising the Lord. "I can do all things . . . through Christ that strengthens me." I bellowed loud and hard with the voice blasting from my stereo. "I can do all things . . . through Christ that strengthens me . . . I can do all things . . ."

After I arrived home and parked the car, I sat silently inside focusing on the message from God's spokesman and thinking about the awesome ways God encourages His children at the exact moment and with the exact things we need. Who else but God could have known what lurked inside?

Just as I popped the key into the lock and pushed the door open, I heard the shrill ring. Saddled with pocketbook, Bible, note tablet, and keys, I stumbled inside, bumping the door closed with my healthy hips. I dropped my belongings on the nearby catchall chair, then ran into the bedroom to answer the phone.

Plopping down on my bed with a thankful sigh, I grabbed up the receiver. "Hello."

"Is this Saundra?" a haughty voice breathed devilishly from the other end of the telephone line.

"Yes, it is." Unable to recognize the strange voice, I listened carefully as I queried back. "Who is this?"

"I just want to tell you that your husband is in love with me," the female voice spewed with wickedness. Still not identifying herself, she ranted on. "You may think you're something because he's married to you, but, sistah, he comes over to my house every day and I'm wearing him out with all this good loving I'm giving him."

Lord Jesus, help me please. As my heart nearly pounded right out of my chest, something inside me whispered, *This battle is not yours . . . it's the Lord's.* Trying to maintain my composure, as well as hold fast to my profession of faith, I flung my hand across my heart, then asked again, "Who is this?!"

"Don't worry about who I am," the voice scolded, then cursed. "You just worry about your two-timing husband. 'Cause I told him I was going to tell you about us and he said he didn't care."

How could he not care? Surely the fact that some Jezebel called my house, gloating over the thrill of sleeping with my husband, bespoke his devotion to me.

Quite disoriented, I admitted more to myself than to her, "I had a feeling that something like this was going on. I asked him several times if he was messing around. And he looked me straight in the eyes every time and swore he wasn't."

"Well, he lied to you, sistah. 'Cause he's been with me since back before Christmas. And if you think I'm lying, I can tell you what kind of drawers he's had on every day for the past week." Her voice escalated, a bit more wicked. "Tell him to let you see how I wore the seat of his drawers out."

I couldn't breathe. I honestly felt like I would crumble to the floor. Even though I'd suspected he was cheating, I'd never imagined anything as foul as this. I couldn't determine if I was more distraught by what she said or the fact that I'd already seen what she'd suggested. A sight similar to something that wood rats have gnawed on for days and days. "Wore out" seemed quite an understatement from what I'd witnessed. She had to have been telling the truth.

After I thanked her for calling—yes, thanked her—and forcing me to see the truth of my adulterous mate, I promised her that God was going to deal with him and her in a way they'd both regret. Tacky or not, I figured I deserved that one.

The moment I hung up from speaking with her, he called. When I told him about the conversation with his *playmate,* why wasn't I surprised that he started rattling off his same old silly lies? Did he think I was stupid?

Barely married a single year and eager to embrace the joys of holy matrimony, I sacrificed everything for the sake of love. And though I had no intention of entertaining infidelity, my life was rudely interrupted by it.

After coming face-to-face with the ills of adultery, I was furious. "I don't want no explanation and I don't want no time to think nothing over. Get your stuff and get out."

Being bombarded by such despicable hush-hush stuff, I felt wounded and I wanted only two things: an attorney and a divorce. "I've made up my mind and I'm not going to change it!"

And I didn't.

God did.

God dealt with me in a way that literally made me sick. "It is unfair for me to have to suffer behind this sort of mess," I cried. "*He* committed adultery. Why am I being chastised?"

God then imparted a profound message to me. "If you will trust Me," He said, "I will smooth out the rough places."

The more God suggested something spiritually sound to me, the more I allowed it to go in one ear and out the other. I rebutted His Word with a list of excuses as long as a widow woman's dream.

"But I keep thinking about all the stuff that's happened," I complained. "Seems like I continue to see his selfish sins running over and over in my mind."

"You are focusing on the wrong thing," God urged. "You must keep your focus on Me. For I will keep in perfect peace those whose mind stays on Me."

So, there I was, caught between a rock and a hard place.

The man who had promised to love and to cherish me, and to

forsake all others for me, had repeatedly been unfaithful to me. And now he expected to receive forgiveness from me?

"I can't!" I kept telling God. "I just can't do it!"

"Yes, you can," He said, coaching me.

"No, I can't."

To be downright honest, I didn't want to do it. I didn't want to entertain a single thought that would dismiss the consequences of this low-down dirty act of infidelity. My desire to make amends in a marriage to a man like this had rightfully withered away.

Nevertheless, God specializes in doing the impossible. He can handle anything. He knows how to address all things.

He lovingly emphasized to me, "You need not try to overcome all these heartaches and pains on your own." He assured me if I would walk in obedience to His Word, He would remove the pain, the stain, and all else that remained.

When God finally steered me into the understanding of His perfect plan, I hibernated in bed for three days and nights trying *not* to change my mind.

While my marriage was not saved in the end, the unerring love of God slowly changed me; lifted up my hung-down head; wiped away all my tears; put a pep in my step; and taught me, one day at a time, how to live by faith. Talk about a revival!

Father God, we thank You for your unchanging love and Your gift of faith, even in the hardest of times. Help keep us in a state of continual revival. All glory and praise unto You, O God! In Jesus's name, amen.

Let Me Laugh

Wanda J. Burnside

Lord, I need to know how to laugh
When I've been kicked in my teeth.
And not let the enemy's plans
Knock me off my feet.

I need to learn to laugh
When things are going wrong,
And remember that things
Will change before too long.

I need to laugh
When I'm going through a test,
For You are there with me
And will give me sweet rest.

I must laugh
When I'm thrown in the dirt,
For You suffered for me
You're acquainted with all my hurts.

Help me to laugh
When I'm on a raging stormy sea,
For I am not alone
You are there and will help me.

I will laugh
And throw up my hands today.
I will give You all the glory,
And give You the highest praise!

Twelve Weeks of Truth —Week Three

From birth I have relied on you;
you brought me forth from my mother's womb.
I will ever praise you.

PSALM 71:6 NIV

DISCUSSION QUESTIONS

1. In "My Own Creation" Sonya Visor talks about wearing a mask. Have you ever worn a mask with your mother? Has she ever worn one with you? Share your best memory of her.

2. If you have children of your own, has your relationship with your mother affected the way you parent? In a good way or a bad way? How would you like to be remembered by the biological and spiritual children God has brought into your life?

3. If something happened to you in your childhood to make you grow up too soon, was your mother aware of it? What is your relationship with your mother like today? Make a commitment to pray for your mother at least once in the coming week.

Pray the prayer below as a group:

Father God, I thank You for my mother. I release and forgive her for any times that I felt she hurt me or failed to protect me. I accept her for who she is, as she is, knowing that You did the same for me. In Jesus's name, amen.

CHAPTER FOUR

THE FORGIVING HOUR

"And when you stand praying,
if you hold anything against anyone, forgive him,
so that your Father in heaven may forgive you your sins."

MARK 11:25 NIV

Though it isn't usually easy to do, forgiving those who've wronged us, even sexually or physically abused us, sets us free. We don't, however, have to trust that person again or even tell them that we have forgiven them. This is a forgiveness that releases us from our pain and allows us to move on. Be wise, however, in how you show your forgiveness to others. In some cases, you may have to forgive from a distance, especially if communication threatens your safety. Ask God for wisdom and consider yourself and your children before initiating contact with anyone who has been abusive to you in the past. You and your scars are a treasure. But that does not mean you should invite more. Your goal is to move into a more healthy, balanced future full of loving relationships, not to gain the approval of the people who have hurt you.

Hurtful people from your past may never ask for your forgiveness, but you can offer it to God anyway, straight from your mouth to the Father's heart. There is an appointed time to heal, a forgiving hour. If God hasn't called you this place yet, prepare yourself. The forgiving hour is always just a prayer away. Oh and what a joyful time of freedom it is!

Divinely Made

Wanda J. Burnside

There are some things
and faces in my life
that should not be.
I cannot allow them
to take over me.
For my good, they are not.
They have evil plans and secret plots.
They will not rule over me!
For when I was born,
I was born free!
Their words are poisonous to my soul.
My life they want to take control.
Lord, rescue me from this mess
for without You,
I am not strong enough I must confess.
I was divinely made in the image of
The Father, The Spirit and The Son
And in my life,
Their will for me will be done!
I have a victorious and divine destiny,
No one will have the rule over ME!

Drowning Must Be a Terrible Way to Die

Dr. Naima Johnston

*When thou passest through the waters, I will be with thee;
and through the rivers, they shall not overflow thee:
when thou walkest through the fire, thou shalt not be burned;
neither shall the flame kindle upon thee.*

Isaiah 43:2 KJV

Drowning is a terrible way to die; breath snatched as dark waters cover you, panic rising as you're claimed by murky cold. I've discovered that you don't need water to drown; you can suffocate in sin if you don't struggle against the undertow.

Markus led me into the deep and I willingly began to drown. I should've known he'd be my death but I ignored the signs and for seven months slept with the devil. Motives hidden, he blinded me to my own worth, oddly, by speaking the truth, telling me that I was beautiful. The water felt good; I didn't even realize it was creeping higher.

It was a crisp, golden autumn day. The warmth from the sun made it perfect for sitting outside. As a graduate student I'd been busy socializing and found myself frantically skimming pages of educational psychobabble before class. On an academic mission, I was officially grown; I had a car, apartment, bills, and had recently vowed that the next man I slept with would be my husband.

When he approached me, Kangol hat cocked to the side, I was oblivious, engrossed in my textbook. I only looked up because he blocked the sun, his body turning light into darkness. Destruction confidently placed his foot on the bench and leaned close with a look of adoration. My perception of the man whose shadow was superimposed over mine in the dying afternoon was confused. I did a quick inventory: huge gold rope chain, gleaming gold teeth, sharply creased pants. I assumed this meant he was a freshman or drug dealer . . . both unacceptable options. But anxious to review his credentials, I situated myself to show I was receptive to his advances.

"Hi," he said with a smile. "You're the most beautiful woman I've ever seen."

Disbelief furrowed my brow. Me beautiful, as fat as I was?

"Seriously," he continued, "I was driving and saw you. You gonna tell me your name or break my heart?"

Flabbergasted, I nervously giggled.

"Can I take you out? You're beautiful."

I was smitten. No man had ever told me I was beautiful. Conflicting voices in my head spoke: "He's a blind liar. He just wants to hit it. He could be an ax murderer!" "Have you ever been on a date?" "Go to class now, don't stop at go, don't collect a fine man!" "Give him your number, he might be the *one*!"

That was the thought that led me into the deep end of the ocean, the possibility that he could be the *one*! I harbored daydreams of the *one*, the one who'd know—despite my extra weight—that I was his missing rib. The one who'd relentlessly pursue, romance, and catch me. A chocolate brother, slim with a bright smile and eyes that captured me on a maybe.

I gave him the digits, writing with a flourish as my girlfriends approached. I was ecstatic when he ignored their petite perfection. He smiled through the introductions, eyes never leaving my face, then, blowing a kiss, he made a suave exit. The plan for my murder was in motion. But what the enemy meant for harm, God would use for good.

On our first date he sauntered forward, peering at me with an intensity that made me afraid. My body ached from tension; he was beautiful and I couldn't comprehend why he wanted me. We went to Irving's for Red Hot Lovers, a pastel eatery with wrought iron furniture and a greasy-spoon menu. He made sure I had the bigger order of fries and multiple refills of Pepsi while asking probing questions: Did I live alone, where was my family, was I dating anyone?

Answering hesitantly, I was unaware that my responses illustrated my own desperation. He uncovered the brokenness hidden in my heart from the long-ago night when I told a man to stop and he covered my mouth, held down my arms, his knees wrenching my legs open as he thrust and I stopped breathing. He sensed my shame from the man who fondled me like we were lovers on a city train. Both episodes had defined who I became, a hopeless, overweight woman who longed to be loved.

The rose he bought me as we walked by starlight sealed the deal. I almost gave away my future for flowers, fries, and a gaze that never wavered. As he smiled down on me, I basked in the possibility of his love. Being hopeless made me vulnerable; I sensed danger but pressed ahead, longing for wholeness.

When he showed me the explicit, obscene pictures he'd drawn of large women, I perceived it as an artist's appreciation for the full figured. When I took him home and he didn't kiss me I was sold lock, stock, and barrel. During those first weeks he insisted we go slowly. It took two weeks to convince him to kiss me, three for him to spend the night, and five for him to take the most intimate pleasures reserved for my husband. In six weeks I was hopelessly in love, my girlfriends in a panic, and his clothes in my closet.

His attention and dismissals were profound; he dogged my steps, then disappeared for weeks until I was crazed with fear desiring to lie drowning in his eyes. When he returned from seeing his hospitalized brother, dealing with his daughter's drug-addicted mother, the mugging that relieved him of my jewelry, the fight that cost him his job, or any other drama that stole his presence from me, I'd rejoice.

Rapidly our sexual relationship became painfully perverse. In bed, he would lock me in his arms, not allowing me to move. He held me immobile and savagely bit me until I bruised purple tinged with teeth marks. All was forgiven when he whispered,

"You're beautiful," and the screaming in my soul would cease. Admonishing me to eat, he said, "I'll leave if you lose weight." I'd eat frantically, understanding that I was settling for conditional love.

Then one day he declared, "I've done something for our future." Thinking he'd gotten a job, I looked anxiously up from my books. He tossed me an empty bank bag.

"What's this?" I shrieked.

"I robbed a bank so we could have a baby."

Hearing the theme from *Bad Boys,* seeing myself on *Cops,* I imagined glass breaking as the SWAT team surrounded us. "What?" I asked stupidly.

"I robbed a bank."

Stunned and afraid, I ran to my bedroom and locked myself in. He pounded on the door as I wailed. What was wrong with me? I was living with a man who claimed to love me yet was beginning to abuse me and claimed to have made me party to a felony.

Eventually I came out and we went to bed. Filled with disgust, I pushed him away and when he made a move on me, I locked myself in the bathroom, screaming. He was on the other side of the door, coaxing, until I returned to bed and submitted to his dangerous love. We never spoke of the stolen money again.

On Thanksgiving, he disappeared and I drove to my mother's, defeated. When I returned he appeared, devastated; his daughter's mother had killed her, and although I pleaded, he forbade me to go to the funeral. Later, I sat with my friend Tammi and shared the tragedy with her while he used Snow in a Can to decorate her windows for Christmas.

Her dry reply increased the acid in my stomach, "Lots of things happen to that man; he takes it all remarkably well."

He smirked through the glass and I knew that I was killing myself. I couldn't admit to Tammi that I'd been harshly woken up the night before, my arms over my head, him pushing me down into the softness of the bed, breathing hard and using no protection. He was a man on a mission staking his claim. If we had a baby, he'd own me, and although I desired his ownership, something held me back from full surrender.

Later that week, he told me the police wanted to question him about the robbery. Shamed by my own complacency and seeing escape, I insisted he turn himself in, but he swiftly disappeared into the night.

After his departure, I cried until my eyes were swollen shut. He was death, but death was what I sought. He didn't care about the fat, so in my madness I prayed, "Lord, send him home." I learned then that I better be careful what I pray for; I just might get it.

My bed was icy, my dreams nightmares, and my heart shattered. Crying, I picked up my dusty Bible and began to read. I didn't understand much of it, but peace permeated my soul. Still I prayed, "Lord, send him home." Then two months later he was there, and in twelve hours he was back in my bed. His story wasn't plausible, but that didn't matter. He said he'd turned himself in and was released on bond. He hadn't contacted me because he didn't want to implicate me or force me to share our personal intimacies.

I felt sick at his return. Was this what I'd prayed for? I continued to read the Bible and share with him what I read. It was strange. I was steeped in sin but sharing with the one who hurt me with his love that Christ was the answer to every question. I didn't realize that the Bible I held in my hand was teaching me to fight the current.

It was as if my eyes were opening and I began to recognize his lies. A slip here, a change in a recapped tale, the reappearance of a ring lost in a mugging. Then on an overcast day we went to the mall like couples do, and on the way home I popped in the one gospel tape I owned and began to sing. He became enraged as songs glorifying God filled the car, and he seemed tormented by the truth exploding through the music.

With deadly calm he asked, "Are you afraid of me?" Before I could answer he continued, "I could kill you, hide your body, and nobody would ever find you." He ejected the tape and serenely drove home.

That was the most terrifying night of my life; afraid of the consequences, I was submissive and silent as he hovered above me, grunting, eyes dark with lust. Drowning, I cried out to the Lord, "There must be more to my life than this!"

In the morning, done and disgusted with me, he left, and I knew my hope was in the Bible I'd been reading. Determined to discover God, I found a church where the Spirit of the Lord lived. I'd confessed Christ before, but no one had taught me that Jesus was all I needed. I plunged into faith, learning about love and redemption. I discovered that God had a plan for me and the devil wanted to stop that plan before it could come to pass. With joy I learned that it didn't matter what I'd done, God loved me and took me in, whispering that I truly was beautiful.

Everyone marveled at my change; I stopped drinking and cursing, and I listened only to gospel music. I traded my Anne Rice and Jackie Collins novels for the Bible and horror movies for Christian television. I became the center of crass jokes told by friends who'd been privy to explicit accounts of my previous lifestyle. Their laughter hurt, but I grew strong in the Lord, drenched in grace and mercy.

Two months later he called and bile rose in my throat.

"Babe," he said slickly, "I want to see you."

With holy boldness I declared, "Meet me at church." The silence that met my invitation was deafening, but the hum of the dial tone was audible victory. He called several times to see if my faith was a fad and each time we spoke, he seemed smaller. I wouldn't budge but told him that the love of Christ had become my life preserver.

During our last conversation, I admonished him to stop, told him there'd be no us, only Jesus and me.

He spat, "I'll never give up. I'll be a credit application in your life; I'll keep submitting, until like the bank you get tired of me asking and approve me, let me reopen my account."

Laughing fearlessly, I said, "You'll never be approved. I'm nobody's bank; your account is overdrawn and closed." Markus never called again.

I focused on surrendering my shame and guilt; I had to learn to accept that Christ made me free from my past. I was constantly crying at the feet of Jesus, my tears an offering poured out before Him. I struggled to forgive myself and slowly learned to see myself as God saw me.

My self-hate had defined my relationship with that man and led me down dark paths chased by grace. He haunted me, and I deceptively remembered that he was good, forgetting the fear, the teeth and the wet, dark eyes that mercilessly watched me drown. I'd wonder how I could've hated myself so much that I jumped blindly into deep waters. It was the power of God that enabled me to walk away from the only man who ever said I was beautiful, that he loved and couldn't live without me, but also that he'd kill me. How many others have heard those same words and stayed to be drowned because they never met Jesus? How many more are abused and dying?

Grace and mercy are awesome and unexplainable. A year later, he dated the overweight mother of one of my preschool students. After she discovered we'd dated she'd flaunt him as if she'd won a prize and I was the loser of the championship. Her daughter gave a jarring account of hedonism at home and her mother smugly told me she was pregnant.

I mused, "But for the grace of God, there go I." Later she said it wasn't his baby, and I prayed for her. Years passed. I saw him in the mall and he stared, ready to hypnotize. I gazed back, uttered a prayer, and turned away, refusing to give the devil his due. As time passed I discovered that his dead daughter was very much alive, that her mother was an abandoned, drug-free, super-sized beauty, and that he'd left my preschooler's mother before the baby was born. And the bank job? Only God knows.

Grace and mercy are awesome and unexplainable. It could've been me, but mercy said no. That dangerous, seductive relationship left me ashamed because he didn't always push me under; sometimes I held my breath and sank. But time, truth, and the unfailing love of Christ have made me clean and free.

The devil wanted a man to be my death and he was, he killed

me, but not in the way he implied he would. I drowned in blood because of him, dying to sin and self-loathing; I drowned and was buried, only to rise again because the Lord called me from the depths of the waters to walk upon them and not drown beneath them.

Father God, we thank You for being with us in the waters and for saving us from drowning. As we are fearfully and wonderfully made, fill us to overflowing with Your living water. In Jesus's name, amen.

Get Wisdom, Get Understanding

Lady Catherine

*Hear counsel, and receive instruction,
that thou mayest be wise in thy latter end.*

PROVERBS 19:20 KJV

Every trial comes with a lesson to be taught—and learned. I always have to remind myself that the better testimony is how God has kept me. It is well to learn from our mistakes and pass what we have learned to the next generation; my prayer is that whoever reads this will profit from this and understand that Father God gives us parents for a reason.

My reason was tall, dark, dressed to the nines. Mother said, "There's something about this one and I can't put my finger on it. He isn't who we think he is." I shrugged my shoulders and thought to myself, *You don't know what you are talking about, Mother. This one is a dream.*

I was in my third year of college and a very popular young lady on campus. I had good friends, both male and female, and was very respected. I started dating this young man. He was very nice to begin with, but then I started noticing some things, like him yelling at me one day when I asked him a question about another young lady.

Hmm . . . I thought he was in a bad mood, but the horror from hell was just beginning to show his true colors. Not much later, we went out one evening and I saw the demon for sure. That night I got my nose broken because I said no. And then I was date raped.

My life was shattered. Not only did I bear that shame, but one day afterward my side felt like I was having an appendicitis attack. I was in so much pain, my mother took me to the doctor, who called me back a week later to see him.

I had known my doctor all of my life, and he sat me down for a lecture, after which he told me I had gonorrhea. That's when I broke and told him what had happened. I left his office that day, February 14, 1974, full of pain.

I was one of the campus queens of an organization, and I was scheduled to receive an honor from them. The whole time they were honoring me, I cried. They thought I was overcome with the roses, candy, and card but I was saying to myself, "Why didn't I listen to my mother?" I felt like the scum of the earth.

The plot thickened, because then the maniac began to stalk me. It took my mother getting involved verbally and almost legally to get him to leave me alone. I had nightmares and walked in a tremendous amount of fear for many years, even after I got married. My husband is a godly man and we have two beautiful sons, and of the many Christian principles we teach them, number one is respect for all of Father God's daughters.

It took a long time for me to be completely healed and to stop having nightmares, but, praise God, every soul tie has been broken. I'm not sure what happened to him, except that he spent some time in a mental hospital. For the last twenty years I've prayed for his soul, hoping that he has a personal relationship with the Lord and Savior Christ Jesus. I can pray like that because I'm free; I forgave myself and the perpetrator. Remember, wisdom is the chief thing. Walk in it and with all your getting, get understanding. Agape and shalom!

Father God, we praise Your wisdom and the counsel of mothers. Thank You for freedom and forgiveness. Give us eyes to see and ears to hear what the Spirit is saying as we raise up the next generation. In Jesus's name, amen.

I Loved a Boy

Claudia Mair Burney

The sacrifices of God are a broken spirit: a broken and a contrite heart, O God, thou wilt not despise.

PSALM 51:17 KJV

He was an amazing boy. Bright and warm like the sun, and just as beautiful. I remember the first time I saw him. I thought to myself, "He's out of my league. What could he possibly see in me?" Let me tell you, if it starts with you feeling unworthy of him . . . it's gonna end badly.

He was my first.

I remember that day with startling detail. I was afraid. I had prayed about it, and I knew that it was not the Lord's will. Our love was a green shoot, fragile and newborn. It didn't matter that I loved him fiercely. Sex is a God thing. It is holy and full of a mystery that we mere mortals may never fully understand this side of heaven. Things happen in that joining that are complex, and I was not ready for the peril that would assault my soul through that kind of premature loving. The night before, all night long, the Lord troubled my sleep with nightmares. When the Lord talks to you all night in dreams to warn you of danger ahead, and you fail to heed His call . . . it's gonna end badly.

He broke my heart.

Rich Mullins writes, "When you love, you walk on water, just don't stumble on the waves." Not only did I stumble, I was overcome by them. I nearly drowned, and I washed up on the gritty shore of grief, choking and gasping for air. The loss of him, the boy I loved—my sun—devastated my delicate heart. It was two years before the raw and throbbing ache was dulled so that I could bear it. Then I tucked my sorrow deep within my heart. Oh, children of God, don't hide your grief. It will demand release, and the God who loves you will require you to surrender it to Him.

The boy returned.

Only he was a man, and I was a woman. We met, wouldn't you know it, on the Internet. Kids, don't try this at home. Almost immediately, I became a lunatic. Did you know that many waters cannot quench love? Did you know that love remembered is love just the same? Did you know that unresolved grief can render you temporarily insane? Did you know that unforgiveness will eat away at your soul, and bitterness will reveal the ugliest parts of you when you least expect it?

Did you know that God loves you, children? And His love will compel you to come, yes, even with your ragged heart and dirty mind? I know these things. God is good, and if you are in need of a sudden and unexpected mercy, He will give you one, even if you resist it.

That boy! His voice on my phone—a gift, a sudden and unexpected mercy. A grace. The boy I loved on the phone, saying that he loved me. He always loved me! Always would. I was his heart, but he was afraid back then. And I had hurt him, too. He looked for me. For years he asked about me, but that door had closed. And now, my sun had returned, illuminating the dark night of our shared history. I had my first love back. This was amazing! He had spoken and the virgin that was lost inside my heart was released.

I was seventeen again and broken because I had surrendered all to show him that I loved him. He was twenty again and was sorry that he hurt me. Oh, sisters, his voice on the phone, filling the fissures in my heart with, at long last . . . love. This was healing, and how I cried and cried. It should have been enough. It would have been enough, but there was just one thing.

That virgin was mad.

I didn't know she was that angry until she (and I) proceeded to act the fool. My thoughts became consumed with a singular desire. *Return.* I wanted that day back, or at least one like it. *Give me another, a day for a day. One day with you, baby; I'll settle for two hours. I am not a girl anymore. I am irresistible. I am unbreakable. I will make you want me. Shall we trade? Here is the crippling rejection, give me your lust. Boy of my youth, return with me and I will leave you breathless with wanting. Wanting me. I will leave you . . . I will leave you. Before you leave me.*

Uh-oh. The heart really is deceitful above all things and desperately wicked. At least mine is! "Who can know it?" the scriptures ask. But there was another presence in my heart, with a passionate interest in that lost and angry virgin. He loved her, too. And He was a jealous lover, and His voice, the Lover of her soul, was saying to her heart, "My beloved, he is not your first love, *I am.*"

We are never alone. We have never been alone. The God who loves us, the counter of sparrows, He who dresses the lily in splendor . . . He is in Love with us.

"I was there," He says.

"I really hope that's not true, Lord."

"I was with you that day. I was with you the night before, pleading with you in your dreams. I didn't want you to be hurt."

"I got hurt."

"I know. I was there."

And then He asked me for something. "Return," He said. "Give Me that day, and I will heal you."

"Hold it. Now you're asking for too much. I can't give you that day. That was a *bad* day."

"Go back with me. I will show you I was there."

"Lord, I don't particularly want you there. Again, it was a *bad* day."

"Then let Me redeem it. Let Me heal it."

"No."

"I know you are afraid."

"Yes. I am. So leave me alone."

"I never leave you alone. I'm in love with you."

"Stop it."

"*I am.*"

"I know what Your name is, Lord."

"*I am* in love with you."

"I know."

"You don't know."

"Can we talk about this later?"

"That day—give it to me. It's time."

"I really don't think it's a good idea."

"You offered it to *him*."

"That's different."

"He is not the one who can change things. *I am*."

"You know, that whole '*I am*' thing really works for You."

"I know. Don't try to change the subject."

"Why do I argue with You? You know everything. It's an unfair advantage."

"I know that you need healing. So give."

"Awwwwww."

"Give it to Me."

"I'm ashamed of it."

"Do you remember what I said about making your bed in hell?"

"Yes. I've made a lot of beds in hell. I'm a regular chambermaid in hell."

"No, you're not."

"I am."

"Hey, that's *my* Name."

"Sorry."

He stretched out His arms and nail-scarred hands. "I love you. Give me that day."

And I stopped fighting and free-fell into His embrace.

We walk into the stately brownstone, Jesus and me. It is a big, empty house and I joke, "I should have gone for the hotel the boy offered."

Jesus doesn't laugh.

There is a dusty old mattress on the floor, and a blanket. The boy and I are there. I turn to Jesus. "Look how young I look," I say, surprised that I am pretty.

"You were young. You couldn't vote for another two months."

"He is so handsome," I say, and sadness settles into my throat.

Jesus takes my hand in His.

I cannot control the urge to cry. I whisper, "Jesus." For a while, the name of Jesus is all I can say. Jesus holds me and rocks me. He is tender. He is crying, too.

Finally my tears subside. "Lord, I really loved him."

"I know you love him."

"Will I always?"

Jesus looks at me, and the love in His eyes takes my breath away. "Yes, but it won't hurt anymore." He beckons me to look.

The room is illuminated. There are angels all around.

"Angels?" I groan. "Don't tell me there were angels."

"There are always angels," He says.

I watch. The boy and I are on the mattress and he is kissing me. Soon it will happen. I won't be a virgin anymore, and I won't be his wife either. I say to Jesus, "I can't look at this." There is a difference, though. I'm not seeing this as some weird "this is your life" scene from hell. Jesus is here, and I am seeing this from the perspective of eternity.

I close my eyes and I become the girl on the mattress. There are these awkward movements and my body does things that embarrass me. I am horrified. The boy makes a joke to reassure me, but I don't feel better. I experience all that I did on that day—every feeling, mental, physical, and spiritual—only it's different. I know that Jesus is here.

The angels avert their eyes.

Jesus speaks to me. "It is a mystery, and even now, I will not reveal the whole of it to you. You became one with him, and he with you. This is how it has been since creation. You will not understand for many years what took place here, but you will feel its impact for the rest of your life. It will shape your sexual history and how you feel about yourself. This is why I had to bring you back here. This moment changed your life."

There is pain. I wonder what I am doing. How did I get here? It hurts so much. My hands try to push the boy away and he asks me if I want him to stop.

I do.

The boy says something to me that is uncharacteristically

mean. Everything changes for us. If you didn't know your heart can break in an instant, let me tell you that it can. A breath escapes my mouth, carrying with it an unintentional prayer.

Jesus says, "You told me you were sorry in that breath."

"But I didn't say anything," I said.

"I heard what your heart said. I speak the language of sighs and tears."

Then I am standing with Jesus again. I look back at the two kids on the mattress, and He is with them, too. He has his arms around both of them, and I am glad that Jesus is there for the boy, too. He draws the girl closer. He whispers in her ear, "You are forgiven. I love you. I died for this sin. You must forgive yourself now. You must forgive the boy. It is time."

The floodgates open, and I can't stop crying again. "You are forgiven." Jesus says this to me, again and again.

I find myself transformed. I am wearing a white dress, and I am the virgin bride of Christ awaiting my Bridegroom.

I am back now. There is water. I am standing on an ocean of love. The waves are quite manageable, beloved. I am walking on water. I am forgiven. I forgive the boy. I begin to laugh because in the light of eternity, this is such a tiny thing, and yet it is big enough for God to care about. Thank you, Jesus, counter of the hairs on my head. Thank you, Jesus, my First Love and the Lover of my soul.

I am so happy that I dance. The angels dance with me.

Daughters of the Lord, put on your blood-washed dancing gowns, and dance on water with me, for we are forgiven. Praise God, we are forgiven.

Father God, we thank You that we are forgiven. We praise You for taking all our bad days and showing us that, even then, even now, You are with us. Give us the grace to forgive ourselves and others that we might walk on the water and into Your arms. In Jesus's name, amen.

Twelve Weeks of Truth —Week Four

Bear with each other and forgive whatever grievances you may have against one another. Forgive as the Lord forgave you.

COLOSSIANS 3:13 NIV

DISCUSSION QUESTIONS

1. In Claudia Mair Burney's "I Loved a Boy," who does she have the hardest time forgiving? Why is it so hard for her to imagine God being present when she lost her virginity?

2. The stories in this chapter show women who came close to loving a man more than God, more than themselves. These women have spiritual scars but escaped the relationships that once held them captive. Have you ever had a toxic relationship? An abusive relationship? How did you get away?

3. Though your experiences may differ from those in this chapter, we have all been hurt by ourselves and by one another. In some cases, we have even been abused by men we once thought loved us. Forgiving ourselves and others is empowering. We can make our own peace without the other person having to know, especially if it isn't safe to be around them.

Pray the following prayer together:

Father God, I forgive every man who has hurt me mentally, physically, emotionally, or sexually. I release them so that I can take hold of your blessings with both hands. As You heal my brokenness, heal theirs as well. In Jesus's name, amen.

CHAPTER FIVE

TAMAR'S FLIGHT

Tamar put ashes on her head and tore her long-sleeved garment
which was on her; and she put her hand on her head
and went away, crying aloud as she went.

2 SAMUEL 13:19 NASB

Running with nowhere to go. It's a common theme for many women. Though there really is somewhere to go, someone to help, you can't see it for trying to hide. Trying to avoid the look of pity and judgment you've seen too many times before. But sometimes, the choice is taken away and we are thrust out, pushed into a corner. Forced to run so we can rest up and stay alive.

Finding the courage to leave before coming to that point is even harder. Sometimes it seems impossible. And yet, the Father is waiting to help us, to protect us, to bring us home. The angels are prepared to rejoice at the sight of us coming up the road, despite our torn clothes and loud weeping. God knows what has come before. He's been here all the time. Run to Him, Sistah. Run all the way home.

A Woman's Worth

Delores M. Jones, LMSW, MSW

*Indeed, the very hairs of your head are all numbered.
Don't be afraid; you are worth more than many sparrows.*

LUKE 12:7 NIV

I didn't want it to get out. I was too embarrassed. Too educated. Too intelligent to allow this to happen. I really wanted to dance around the issue. I didn't want others to see him differently. Or did I? Was I really protecting him? "No," I told myself. "You are not judging him for what happened and this is the Christian thing to do, right?"

Everything was in black and white. His e-mail read, "My hitting you had nothing to do with your hitting me in a great sense. It was the frustration of having to prove myself and my love and commitment to you every step of the way. It was the frustration of not hearing I love you or I miss you or I appreciate you and all of the big and little things that I do for you and all of the sacrifices that I make to make you happy. The frustration of not being enough, like I was inadequate. It was the frustration of feeling disrespected and unloved by the person who vowed to love me and cater to me."

In his own words he described what had been in his heart for some time that lead to the big blow. What he described as hitting, others—police and EMTs—called domestic assault. His fist had cut my lower lip, severed parts of my top gum, and dislocated my left front tooth. Prior to this, my teeth were perfectly straight, my smile radiant, and my lips full and beautiful.

When the police and hospital nurses began questioning me about what had happened, I mumbled the words, "I was punched in the mouth." I could not believe that I had just said "punched" and "I" in the same sentence.

As I lay there on the hospital bed, I kept thinking about the fact that only a year ago I had left him. It was clear to me, based on behavioral patterns and incidents that I knew so well, that this relationship was not healthy and potentially violent.

Hadn't I had spent time counseling other women about the "power and control wheel" that helps the abused see the patterns of abuse? I had served on the board of directors for a battered women's shelter. I'd even interviewed experts and victims about domestic violence on my very own radio talk show and published an article on the subject in the local newspaper. I had earned a master's degree in social work and focused my attention on women's issues.

And yet, I was in an ambulance, bleeding.

I had just returned from Chicago for a taping of *The Oprah Winfrey Show*. Yes, only eighteen days before the assault, he had accompanied me to Chicago to watch a dream of mine come true. Dr. Bill Cosby had included excerpts from my personal story in his book *Come On, People: On the Path from Victims to Victors*. As a result, one of Oprah's producers had called to interview me. During the show, Cosby asked me to stand up and introduced me to Ms. Winfrey as her replacement. Honored and humbled by his declaration, I tried my best to retell my story from Dr. Cosby's book in a way that conveyed my conviction of faith and commitment to education despite homelessness and the murder of my birth mother, Mary Ann Jones, when I was just five years old.

I had just watched a dream of mine come true. So how did I miss it? Why was I lying on a hospital bed with a doctor inserting a needle in my lip to close up a cut that would require at least two stitches?

When the hospital social workers came in to take pictures I tried to use humor to cope with the obvious. I said, "Well, as the swelling goes down, I can pretend that I had a Botox treatment. After all, it is what some of the celebrities are doing these days." They laughed slightly, as did my great-aunt Joyce and colleague Paulette. Paulette and Joyce were the two people I called because I knew they loved me and would not judge me. I knew they were there to make me feel better, but I was in pretty bad shape and it would be a miracle if the dentist could save my tooth and restore my smile.

I met with two dentists that day and they too wanted to know what had happened. Trying my best to hide the embarrassment, shame, and brokenness, I said, "I was punched in the mouth." Both of them shook their heads in disbelief. Perhaps each of them had seen this sort of thing before, but I dared not ask. I was in too much pain from them pushing and applying pressure in order to reposition my tooth. The pain was excruciating. The long needles injected in my gums to numb me were almost unbearable. I said a silent prayer, "Lord, please save my tooth."

I wanted to smile again. I needed to be able to do my radio show, give lectures to the social work class I was teaching at the community college, and give instructions to the high school and middle schoolers I taught two to three times a week. Most important, I had promised my nine-year-old son that I would take him to the WWF (World Wrestling Federation) event that was happening in just three days.

A miracle happened. One dentist could save my tooth, but I would be required to wear a tooth guard during the day and while I slept. I would also undergo a root canal and fitting for a crown. The process would take five to ten visits to the dentist's office within a two-to-three-month period. In the meantime, I watched my once white tooth turn brownish gray. The dentist said the discoloration occurs when there has been trauma to the nerve. "Oh, no. I'm not ready for this. Someone will notice," I told myself.

I did my best not to smile as big. The day I took my son to the wrestling event, I wore a mask that people use to keep the dust out. I told my son that I had gone to the dentist and that my mouth was sensitive. I never told him what had happened. When they dimmed the lights in the arena I lowered the mask so I could breathe better.

"Why does it hurt so bad? Why do I feel so sad?" Whitney Houston's words played in my head as I confronted my own contradictions about love and abuse. The heartache of letting go of someone you once loved is daunting, and at times I tried to find loopholes to hold on to the love we once had. James Baldwin said, "You cannot fix what you will not face." In order for me to do this I had to be willing to let go of what once was and see it for what it currently was. Willingness is also about truth.

In reading John 8:32, I also understood, "And ye shall know the truth, and the truth shall make you free." Nothing about what I had experienced at the hands of the man who had said he loved me promoted freedom. Instead it brought fear. If I was completely honest with myself, there were countless other behaviors and actions that told me this was not love. I had chosen to make excuses about his infidelity while we were separated. I even chose to ignore stories of abuse from women in his past.

Even with all this, I returned home to him. In the end, I left him a final time, but I left the door open for him to come to me. Later, when I started to mentally beat up on myself, I was reminded that on average, a woman will leave an abusive person seven times, sometimes losing her life in the process. With this in mind, I realized my desire for him was normal, but I had a son to raise, an example to set, a God to serve.

I needed to know my own worth.

Father God, thank You for calling us priceless, for offering the best You had to redeem us—Your own Son. May all of our actions and choices be those of women who know their worth. In Jesus's name, amen.

Going Home

Dorien Hage

"Return home, my daughters."

RUTH 1:11 NIV

The bare lightbulb laughed at me from above the garage. There in the driveway, I sat in my Buick gripping the steering wheel in defiance, already late for work because earlier I'd ironed his shirt while he huffed and puffed over my shoulder at each imperfect crease.

I *needed* that light when I came home from my job. I put the car in reverse but stopped. If I didn't leave the light on, I'd be staggering through the dark in this neighborhood with my purse, my lunch box, the diaper bag, and my baby girl in her infant carrier.

But if I left it on, he'd know.

Then everything would be my fault—the electric bill we couldn't pay, the supper not cooked like his mama's, the house having holes in the Sheetrock, whatever. Everything was my fault—stupid, ugly, unlovable, ungrateful. Thought I was better than everyone else; just look at me. Lucky to have a man like him to put up with my sorry self.

I believed every word.

Why was I so afraid? I worked. My money paid the bills just like his. Didn't he want his wife and child to walk in the light to the safety of their home? Again, I put the car in reverse, then park. Rather than risk the chance of him catching me or my breaking my own neck in the dark later that evening, I pulled my sweater over my hand, like an oven mitt, and unscrewed the lightbulb. A lie. A necessary little twist by a hand covered with green cable-knit fear.

What happened to me? When did I become this timid Lifetime movie wife?

First-generation high school graduate? First-generation college graduate?

What a joke!

Working as a clerk so he'd feel better about himself, Mr. Breadwinner. And my parents so proud of me, living in a brick home, working at a real nice job with benefits and a retirement. More than they ever expected from me. What would they think if they knew what really went on?

That weekend, I placed my fussy daughter in her car seat and drove around town, looking at other houses with pink petunias in their front yards. Did those wives fear holes in the wall? Were they lucky? Could they afford meat at the grocery store and a dry cleaning bill? Or did they duck the flying iron when the creases weren't just right?

Another day I gripped my chipped teddy bear coffee mug at the kitchen table, listening to another tirade. Ungrateful. Stupid. Lucky. All because I got in the shower before him when our alarm clock didn't wake us on time.

Another hole in the wall.

Don't be here when he got home. He wouldn't be responsible for what happened to me. I didn't ask what he meant, knowing my green sweater wouldn't protect me this time. No pot holders could shield me from the heat. What was I gonna do?

The chipped teddy bear mug had no answers.

He had the checkbook. He had gotten my credit cards canceled, by using them and purposefully not paying the bills. Our savings? The credit union already told me I wasn't on the account and needed his signature for a withdrawal. I'd checked his wallet for cash the night before. All I found was a couple of ones, women's phone numbers scribbled on miscellaneous scraps of paper, and charges to my parents' gas card they'd given me "just in case of emergencies."

What would my parents think?

After he left, I pulled on my pink sweats, called in sick, and took my baby girl to day care.

Now what?

I couldn't think straight, so Crazy Woman took over. That today, she made sense.

The baby needed formula. And I needed a cigarette. He hated it when I smoked. Wal-Mart. Enfamil, Pampers, pink Easter dress, white rhumba tights, hamburger, chicken breasts, T-bone steaks, potpourri, *Country Living* magazine, L'Oréal Passion lipstick, avocados, pita bread, Hanes Her Way size six, a white blouse, twelve-packs of Coke Classic, Folgers, and so much stuff we can't afford . . .

And a carton of Virginia Slims menthol lights.

I laughed when the cashier told me the total and reached for my—

Checkbook?

Where was my purse?

Must have left it in my Buick. Nervous giggle. Told her I'd be right back.

Walking toward the car, my feet hurt. I looked down. No shoes. Had lost mind. Laughed so hard I began to cry. People stared at me in the parking lot. Crazy Woman drove off, paid cash for a pack of cheap cigarettes at a gas station, went home, and made another pot of coffee. Smoked the whole pack in an hour, trying to catch enough snap to make plans.

The clock ticked above me, to my right. He'd be home in two hours for lunch. I was supposed to be at work. No sick time. My paycheck would be short. We really wouldn't be able to afford the light bill. He'd smell the smoke. Holes.

What would my parents think?

Below the clock, the buff-colored phone shone as a beacon.

Deep breath. *Pick up the receiver, dial, and ask for the extension . . .*

"Hello?"

"Mom! I need to come home. Don't ask." *Please don't think anything.*

"Are you okay? Is the baby okay?"

They know! I swallowed. "Yes. She's at the day care."

"Go get her now and come home."

"What does Daddy think?"

"Don't worry about that—just come home now."

Seconds later, I ripped white tall kitchen trash bags from the roll and ran for the baby's room, cramming in the baby clothes in huge pink wads. What kind of mother didn't have her baby's things? *Hurry!* Somehow, I managed to stuff her crib and all her things into my Buick in under five minutes.

The baby's medicine!

I raked my arm through the cabinet, knocking bottles, tubes, and tubs of Tylenol, PediaCare, baby Anbesol, A+D Ointment, Vicks VapoRub, Biaxin into another trash bag. Then I started for the door. Behind me, the phone rang. I froze.

It's him. He knows.

I let it ring, ring, ring, ring . . . twenty-five times. My age. Crazy Woman laughed.

It could be the day care.

What kind of mother didn't answer the phone? I walked toward it, picked it up, and put it to my ear without a word, knowing I could hang up if I heard the familiar sounds from his job—people yelling, phones ringing, lives outside the law.

No sounds. Only quiet. No holes in the wall. My wall.

"Honey?"

"Mom?"

She's changed her mind. She's talked to him. I'm crazy. They're coming for me.

"Your daddy's on his way, he'll be there any second."

Father God, sometimes we're so lost, we can't even begin to see our way home. Guide us, Lord. Show us. Point us in the direction we are to go. And we'll do our best to follow. In Jesus's name, amen.

How Dare You

Robin Caldwell

And the second is like it: Love your neighbor as yourself.
MATTHEW 22:39 NIV

He burst through the door like gangbusters and ran in, only to stop dead in his tracks at the sight of the police. One officer was kneeling on the floor in front of me, examining my face, while the other officer, a woman, sat beside me rubbing my back as I sobbed.

"Robin, I'm sorry," he stammered, looking not once at me but at the officer, the man with his hand on the butt of his revolver.

The officer, the man, said, "Sir, did you do this to her?"

"I refuse to answer on the grounds that it may incriminate me." He had attended law school and knew to plead the fifth.

Yet he continued talking. "It was the devil. The devil did this, Robin."

Through my tears I said, "The devil didn't do it, you did."

My heart thumped in my chest every bit as loudly as it had while he beat the living daylights out of me. I had been prone, lying on my right side with my eyes closed because I had a headache. He just gave me another one.

We were babysitting for friends in their apartment and he was going through their personal things, saying he would use their laundry detergent to wash his clothes. I thought that was flat-out wrong and asked him not to do it.

Bam!

My heart thumped the same exact way it had when he sent my head flying into a cinder-block wall when I tried to run from him. The only time my heart hadn't thumped was as I slid down that wall and I heard the voice of Bunny, my spiritual mom, telling me, "If he lays a hand on you and you don't try to kill him,

I'm killing you." It seemed like Bunny knew before I did that he'd ultimately hit me.

By the grace of God or the fear of Bunny, I stood up, slowly using my hands to guide me up that wall and push me away from it to walk briskly past him to hunt down a butcher knife in the kitchen.

I was about to kill the dude, because Bunny wasn't killing me. "You don't get it; I'm about to kill you." I wasn't a street girl, but I knew that when a person turns his or her back to you, they are not afraid or they no longer care. I was no longer afraid. Without flinching I returned to my hunt.

He must have inherently understood what it meant when a person, this woman, didn't have any fear. For months he'd used my fear to say some of the most hurtful and mean things to me; in a sick way that beating felt better than hearing him call me names or tell me how worthless I was and how he'd leave me.

On this night, he must have known I was about to fillet him, because he ran out the door. The blessing that kept me from experiencing three hots and a cot was that my neighbors hid their knives from their toddler daughter. They had moved the knives out of her reach and mine.

Walking over to the door to double-check the lock, I then casually and calmly tiptoed down the hall to check on the toddler in my care who was soundly asleep in the next room. I thanked God because I really don't know what I'd have done if she witnessed that mess—a mess like the ones I'd witnessed as a child.

Yet the fear returned when he walked back through that door. Even though my friend Elizabeth and the two cops were there, my heart thumped. I could feel it and I could hear it. I have no idea why I was scared.

"Robin, I'm sorry—"

"Sir, I need to inform you of your rights. In this state, an apology is an admission of guilt. You have the right to remain . . ."

In less than three minutes, a slightly shorter time than it took for my eye to swell up, my face to turn black and blue on the left side, my head to start throbing even more, he was arrested and in a squad car. He was gone, and my heart still thumped.

My heart didn't stop thumping for several days. It banged against the cavity of my chest, thumping truly hard when it sensed impending danger or was reminded of the beating I took.

It thumped uncontrollably that same night as my telephone rang and rang and rang; members of our church continually called to get the facts and then ask if I was okay. I was an afterthought. Conversations went like this: "Hello, Robin. I heard he's in jail. What happened? What did you say to him to make him . . . ? When did it happen? Oh, yeah, are you okay?"

The next day I put on makeup over the bruises, but it's truly hard to cover black and blue and red and eggplant with Fashion Fair Honey Glo foundation. Honey Glo covers a multitude of skin sins, but not fresh bruises and scars from a beating.

I needed some things from the grocery store, so I wore the Honey Glo anyway and a pair of Ray-Ban sunglasses, and pretended no one could tell I had been beaten to a bloody pulp. That was my little secret. *Wink wink.*

As I stood in the checkout line, a man who had no concept of personal space reached over me, and I almost beat him with that plastic bar used to separate purchases. My heart thumped so loudly, I was sure he could hear it too. I was too ashamed and even prideful to explain why I jumped, but I had no qualms about telling him to back the you-know-what up. It just flowed out of my mouth too easily and a little too carelessly, but I didn't care even if I was supposed to be saved.

The man who beat me was saved too; he was a church deacon. I surmised that if he who was saved could beat the snot out of me, then I who was saved could cuss.

We were even.

My pastor called to tell me that all lovers have spats. "It was just a little fight that went too far," he said. I laughed, heart thumping louder and louder, as he continued on and on about forgiving, forgetting, and oh yeah, "Could you drop the charges?" Keeping my mouth shut tight, I just listened, perhaps giving the impression that I agreed with him.

"Come on, now. We can work this out. Plus, we need you at church. You were doing such a great job of planning my anniversary."

To this day, I'm not sure if he actually said that to me or if I'd only imagined he had, because it seemed like the most absurd and audacious thing to say to a woman who couldn't eat or brush her teeth because her "lover," the man she had the "spat" with, pummeled her face. I just hung up.

My heart thumped when his mama and daddy called, his best friend called, and a battery of church folks called. But I actually thought it would jump out of my chest when one minister called and told me that if I didn't drop the charges, I'd be just "another black woman working with the man to kill off brothers." My heart raced and thumped on that one, and it should have, because this was a man married to a white woman, and he, in that one remark, had unknowingly shared why he wasn't with a sister.

I took the phone off of the hook.

Even when the swelling went down and the bruises went away, I felt like they were there like blemishes from a bad breakout—really huge black marks. If it only took a few days for those to disappear, it would take much longer for the blemish of shame to disappear from my spirit.

Honestly, we were living in a small university town and most of the black folks knew one another. It was like being in high school, walking around knowing tongues were wagging but having no energy to defend against or control the murmurings.

When an article appeared in the student newspaper, I was devastated and retreated to my apartment, calling off class and work obligations. I begged for time off just so I could lie in the fetal position on the couch, stare at the television, and ask God why He allowed this man to beat me. I was special, right? So why would He allow this man to beat me?

God is sovereign and in control. He is also all-knowing and

all-seeing. He knew this man would beat my behind long before I did, so why did He allow it? In my battered mind, I decided that God felt I deserved to be beaten. End of story.

And yet, it was only the beginning of the story. I figured that God allowed the beating for the same reason He had allowed me to have been molested and beaten as a child. I believed that I was born to be abused, someone created to be hurt. I had little evidence to believe otherwise. That was my lot in life and I needed to simply accept it. So after a while I stopped asking why and declared, "I get it now."

In getting my understanding, I cut my shoulder-length hair to less than a quarter of an inch from my scalp. You could see the skin on my head. I stopped going to church, reading my Bible, praying, and hanging out with the folks from church. I watched the movie *The Color Purple* three times in a row one day, crying at every indignity suffered by Celie and Sofia.

For months, I lied to my family and friends at home when they asked about him, telling them that he was fine and yes, we were still planning a wedding. They, after all, had articulated on many occasions that I could not keep a man, and when it came to arguments I was always the cause—always.

So when I tired of lying, I devised an elaborate plan to announce that we'd broken up. It would start with minor complaints and end with the declaration, *He got on my last nerve,* to which my family would say, *It figures.* And that would be the end of that; I'd take the weight of a lie over the weight of the truth.

How could I say, "I broke up with him because he beat my butt. That's why!"

God knows I would have loved to have said that to someone in my family, but I didn't think they'd care enough to give me what I thought I needed, which was to be defended and protected. If God didn't defend or protect me, then why would my relatives?

Ultimately, I tired of being rebellious and angry and decided to be civil with God, though I still believed that He created me to be beaten and abused. It would take years before I stopped believing that. But for the sake of a peaceful coexistence, I decided to be civil. It was His world after all and I needed Him for fundamentals such as breathing.

Marketia, my sister in spirit and friend, had recently received Christ as Lord and Savior, and on the occasion of her marriage to Marcus, she witnessed so sweetly and innocently to me about forgiving the God I'd introduced to her and of whom I'd spoken so lovingly before the beating. It was at her urging that I decided to forgive the Lord and move forward.

Shortly thereafter, in the quiet of my home, I was sitting in my living room; I heard the voice of God for what I believed to be the first time in my life. It was so clear, and so distinct from any voice I heard in my head—the voice I called my thoughts. He said, "How dare you think less of yourself than what I think of you, Robin?" And for the years to follow, even now, He has lovingly and painstakingly shown me what that means. I'd be the first to admit that I am not an expert, but I get it enough to negotiate my way through those situations testing my worth and value.

I now refer to that evening when I got my butt whipped as the night that man knocked some sense into my head. Actually, to be more precise, he drove a point directly to my brain that would eventually travel to my heart and my spirit: *I am worth more than this . . .*

The day before he drove that point home, I sat in a Christian counselor's office, pouring my heart out to her about the abuse I'd suffered as a child and all of the damaging sins I'd committed as a result. I'd told her, "My boyfriend says I need help. I'm here because he said that I have problems."

She stopped me in midsentence and said as matter-of-factly as possible, with tears welling in her eyes, "You're not the one with the problem, honey. It's him." I ignored her and kept droning on about how he had to restrain me one evening, lock me in his bedroom, because I was hard to control.

She stopped me once again and said, "Honey, don't do that. It's him who has the problem, not you." Then she threatened to end our session if I didn't listen—really listen.

I listened.

On the night he drove the point home, I finally understood what she meant. The things he'd said and done to me before that beating had set the stage and were actually more damaging than those punches. Still, today, I thank that man for beating me and being a willing participant in my abuse and ultimate spiritual and emotional growth. If he had not followed his instincts, I would have never understood that God follows His. And one of the Father's instincts is to protect us from ourselves; only He knew what I'd do to me or would allow to have done to me had I not been driven to the point of truly caring for myself and this life He had made me a steward of.

I tell people all of the time, because I can and because I know firsthand: We hear Jesus when He says, "Love your neighbor as you love yourself," but we fall short at the "love yourself" part. We do not—I did not—know what it means to love ourselves.

I honestly thought loving myself meant exercising and staying away from smoking, drinking, and dancing the hoochie-coo. I protected my temple in those ways, or I tried. But I didn't protect my temple from verbal, emotional, and spiritual abuse because I didn't think I could or should. I honestly didn't think I had to; that was God's job, and I'd initially believed that He failed to protect me, like my family had failed to protect me.

Before that beating, I had plenty of opportunity to get out of that relationship, but I stayed and stayed because I wanted to stay. At the heart of my staying was a sense of unworthiness. It wasn't until that night the Lord said, "How dare you . . . ," that I got the memo and rose to retrieve His love letter to me and find out what it meant to think of myself as He thought of me.

And thank Him; He thinks more of me than I could have ever thought to think of myself.

Father God, Thank You for sending us Your love letters, for daring us to see ourselves as You see us—royal and radiant. Bring us beauty as we share our ashes. Give us the courage to dare to love ourselves. In Jesus's name, amen.

Twelve Weeks of Truth —Week Five

From the ends of the earth I call to you,
I call as my heart grows faint;
lead me to the rock that is higher than I.

PSALM 61:2 NIV

DISCUSSION QUESTIONS

1. In "Going Home" by Dorien Hage, what was she most afraid of? Were her fears substantiated? What do think might have happened if she had stayed?

2. The women in this chapter had to discover their own worth in the sight of God before they could make the decision to get out of dangerous situations. Have you ever had to ask God for the courage and strength to leave someplace or someone? Discuss within the group.

3. As in the verse above, sometimes our hearts grow faint in trying to figure out what to do. Think back over your life to a time when God guided you and write it down in your testimony notebook.

Pray this guidance prayer as a group:

Father God, grow me. Know me, Lord. Show me where to walk. May nothing I do in word or deed diminish the price You paid for me: the blood of Your own Son. Put my feet on pleasant paths, in the name of the One who Keeps us from falling. In Jesus's name, amen.

CHAPTER SIX

THE HEALING PEN

My heart is overflowing with a good theme;
I recite my composition concerning the King;
My tongue is the pen of a ready writer.

PSALM 45:1 NKJV

Though some of the things that have hurt us took things away, many women find that they begin writing as a means of healing. For some, it is the writing of letters to the person who hurt them (not to be mailed, but just to release). For others, it is behind the words of stories or articles that they find comfort. Though we may start out writing for deliverance, in the end we are writing about the King.

Life's Reintroduction

Carmita McWebb

It took some time to get here,
time to discover what our lives really mean.
And now that we know who we are . . .

We can speak death to mountains of fear
and dance on clouds of hope.
We can call ourselves champions and take a ride
on the white horse of victory.
We can fly to every corner of the earth,
joyfully shouting on the rooftops of nations
WE have been reborn!
We can be proud of who we are . . . anywhere we are . . .
at any time.

For we are the light that shines on the darkness
of every lonely heart.
We are witnesses to those who doubt
the power of truth.

And with Love as our guide,
we can become
Living inspirations . . .

Breathing faith on every open soul.

We control the tides of peace, the ups and downs
of earthly relationships.

Let's take a trip back to the beginning . . .
Back to when we believed we'd succeed at anything.
Let's return to the healthy imaginations of our youth,
before we allowed time to strip us of our patience.

For we are not dead and we are not lost.
We have arrived,
and we have arrived just in time.
It took some time to get here,
time to discover what our lives really mean.
And now that we know who we are . . .

It's time to be strong, time to be bold,
time to know that our words can be heard
across the sea.

It's time to be sure
that we are who we are
because it's the truth
and not what they said we should be.

Don't you agree?
It's time.

Confession Is Good for the Soul

Stanice Anderson

Confess your trespasses to one another,
and pray for one another, that you may be healed.
The effective, fervent prayer of a righteous man avails much.

JAMES 5:16 NKJV

Dear Daddy:

I do so enjoy your letters. I hope you don't mind but after the last family gathering I shared your letters with your grandson, Mike. It made his heart glad to know that you are proud of him. Lately, you have communicated your feelings in letters and verbally that I've always wanted and needed to hear from you. I guess it's natural and normal for a daughter to need validation from her father.

Even as I was growing up I'm sure you loved me, though I don't recall you saying it. But if you did, maybe I was not open to receive the love. My life hurt so much of the time and I wanted to tell you—but I couldn't. I lived in the shadows somewhere between pain and shame. I could not break free no matter how hard I tried. I laughed and attempted to appear normal but the anger—the ache—the secret held me hostage.

Remember the first time I played hooky from school? I was fourteen years old and I just wanted to be like the other girls. I was tired of being different—of being a good little girl. It was too lonely. Well, something happened to me that spring day that forever changed my life. Childhood as I once knew it ended. I awoke a vibrant rose of youth that morning and by afternoon the petals were stolen and stomped on, leaving only the stem of prickly thorns lost somewhere between limbo and hell.

I went voluntarily on a dare with a girl I thought was my friend to Northeast Washington. I had no idea that I would be the virgin that was led to the rim of a volcano and sacrificed to appease the gods. We went to an apartment on Adams Street. There was one guy there who said some other girls were on their way. My friend said that she was going to the store and would be right back. I followed her to the door, but she wanted me to wait there so that I would be there when the other girls arrived.

I nervously sat on the couch as I noticed that the boy looked older than what she told me he was. He attempted conversation and then I heard sounds coming from the back of the apartment. Following the sound were voices—men's voices. Everything happened so fast. Down the short hallway came a man, then another man. That made three men and me. They seemed to scatter out of the walls like roaches when you turn the lights on. I headed for the front door. I don't know who hit me first. Fists pounded into me, hands covered my mouth, and arms pulled my legs. They dragged me into the bedroom.

Then the air filled with cursing and shouted demand. "Shut up! I'll kill you if you scream."

I tried to fight but my legs and arms were pinned to the bed. "Please don't do this," I begged. "I'm only fourteen!"

"Didn't I tell you to shut up? Shut her up, man." Fists, then more fists pounded my face. I could feel my eyes swelling like dinner rolls on a hot day. Everything faded to black. Then lights flickered like strobe lights and comets with endless tails. A combination of excruciating, pulsating hot pain and icy numbness surged through my body.

"Daddy! Daddy! Help me, Daddy!" I cried out to you; but you never heard me. You never came. No one came. No one helped me.

Drowning in a pool of shame, degradation, and pain, I wanted to die. I remember thinking, How can I live with this? How will I explain to my parents or my husband one day that I'm not a virgin anymore? Everyone will know. God, why are you letting this happen to me?

It felt like car doors slamming and smashing every part of my body at the same time. I hid myself as best I could under a fortress of thoughts, prayers, promises, wishes, and anything that would help me not be there in that awful and degrading place, with those horrible and brutal men. And then, like I wished it—it was over. But it would never really be over.

The three men let me go; but I heard one of them tell my girlfriend, "Make her understand that if she tells—she dies!"

What no one could see was that something inside me had already died. My hope in a future and my desire to live through the present, my ability to love and be loved, my trust for anything that breathed—especially men and big girls who pretend to be friends—had died. My belief in God, who the preacher in the pulpit said had promised never to leave me or forsake me? Gone. My belief that I was a worthwhile human being? All murdered and left inside me to rot. I was damaged goods, destined to be alone. Alone with the nightmare. Alone with the pain. Alone with the secret of what happened that spring. The stench began before I could get back home.

For years, I relived that rape almost every night in my dreams. As the nightmares haunted me, my pain turned to anger, which in time gave birth to rage. A red-hot rage directed toward men, who had the capacity to hurt me; women, who had the capacity to betray me; and myself, who had the capacity to let it all happen. I also felt rage toward God for allowing the rape to happen. I vowed never to be hurt again—never to trust again—and never to love God or human beings.

For a time, drugs and promiscuity seemed to help me forget. The succession of men and living life on the edge became my therapeutic solution to kill the secrets that would not die.

In addition, I soon found out that secrets grow in the dark. They fester like a cancer and eat away at the soul.

I chose men who would physically and verbally abuse me and were capable of doing the unspeakable. The dark men. I was raped again and sodomized at seventeen. Raped again at eighteen, and raped and beaten on several occasions by another man whom I was in a relationship with for two years.

At thirty-four, hopelessly addicted to drugs and at what I thought had to be the end of my life, I was in my apartment. I had been in the bathroom shooting heroin in my veins for most of the weekend. Exhausted and sick of myself, I went to the refrigerator to get some Kool-Aid and as I passed by my black and white TV set with the coat hangar antenna, there on the screen was a man talking about his drug addiction. He recalled the disgust he had for himself. He went on about the degradation, broken promises, and endless lies. But when I looked at his face and his demeanor it was evident he was no longer in a hopeless state of being.

Even on my black and white television set, he looked radiant, alive, and full of hope. So much so that it seemed I was seeing this man in living color. His tanned pinkish skin looked smooth and his brown eyes seemed so bright that they appeared to twinkle. I talked to the man on the television screen. "What did you do? How did you get out of the despair so alive and free?"

I forgot all about the Kool-Aid and sat down on my sheetless mattress, which was on the multicolor patched, carpeted floor. I listened and was mesmerized by what I saw and heard. It was as if he heard my questions, because his next words were, "I asked Jesus to come into my life. To forgive me for my sins, to live his life in me."

Desperate and already on the floor, I rolled over onto my knees and prayed the same prayer. It seemed as though a brilliant light flooded my apartment. It was as if the light was God stepping through my apartment door. Still on my knees, I told God all about my life—where it hurt, the bad things I had done and said—everything I could think of came pouring out of my mouth like someone had given me a shot of truth serum left over from the days of the Cold War.

I guess it was in my mind, but it seemed like I heard my name being called: "Stanice." It sounded like a choir of angels hummed my name to a celestial melody. I had long since given up my real name. Most people only knew me as Stacey. Thinking about my real name made me remember who I really was, where I came from, who my parents were. But it hurt too much to remember.

Maybe it was just in my mind and heart, but I recall having a conversation with God that night.

After I poured out my past, it was as if God said, "I know, Stanice. I was with you. I've never left you. I love you. You have been mine from the beginning of time."

Such a sweetness and weightlessness came over me. The fear, the self-loathing, the despair, and the hopelessness drained out of me. It was all replaced with a sense of peace, love, and forgiveness.

But you know me, Dad. I still fought the experience. I just couldn't believe that the God of the universe cared about me and had time for me. I felt that I had gone too far over the edge to be brought back. In my mind, I argued, "But, God, you don't understand. I'm damaged goods," as I remembered the rape.

But every wall I threw up, God seemed to come through. "I'll repair whatever is broken in your life—everything."

No one can tell me that I did not have an experience with God that night. I recalled things that I had desperately tried to forget. The secrets seeped from my lips and died in God's light. I felt like I was being shown with every confession I made that God had me in the palm of His hand from the beginning.

Dad, it had to be God, because these thoughts I had were too insightful and pure for me to have on my own. I sensed Him saying, "I knew you even before you were born. I knit you in your mother's womb. I made you black. I set you in that family. I made you a girl and in the era you were born. Nothing that has been has been by chance. While the boys of your era were being called to Vietnam, your girlness made you exempt. I did that.

"And yes, I knew about the abortions. It was I who gave you the strength to get off that bed and call for help when that woman left you for dead. It was also I who did not allow those men who raped you to kill you. Yes, each time.

"It was I who brought you to consciousness in that infirmary at Fayetteville State when you OD'd on cough syrup. You did see a glimpse of heaven. It was not a dream. I allowed you to come back. When you OD'd on that heroin alone in your office on that Sunday, it was I who reminded the woman who found you that she needed her briefcase and sent her back to the office. You think she just happened by chance to come back and see your keys, know you were there, get the guards, break through the door, and rescue you? No! It was not by chance. It was on purpose—My purpose.

"It was I, your God, who breathed life into your body in the ambulance the three times you flatlined. It was I who reinflated your lung after it collapsed. Once they got to the hospital, it was I who had your cousin Vicki on duty in the emergency room. She recognized you and called your mother."

The thoughts did not let up. "Remember the time you felt your life leaving your body as John beat and choked you? It was I who stopped him before he killed you. And it was I who stopped you from going into that apartment even though you tried three times to put the key in the door. That spark you felt was My Spirit warning you of the danger waiting on the other side of the door. I alerted you to call the police and wait. When the police got there, do you remember they found him in the emptied apartment waiting for you to turn the key and come in? Again you were spared. I have never left you, nor will I ever leave you.

"And it was I that year who got you the temp assignment the day your buddy overdosed on heroin. You know that had you been with her you would have injected yourself first. She died but you lived.

"There have been many washed-out bridges on the roads you chose to take but I navigated you around all of them. Some you know nothing about, but know this, my child, I have a plan for your life. While the evil one meant to harm you, I alone worked all things together for your good."

I found myself no longer wanting to fight. How could I fight such love, compassion, and grace? No one had ever shown me such a love as I felt in those moments. I felt like I had wrestled with an angel and lost. I surrendered and fell over limp on the sheetless mattress, wept, and thanked God. It was that night that my new life with God was born.

Dad, I do want you to know that the rage is gone and I am no longer in bondage to my past. God healed the gaping emotional wounds left by the rape and enabled me to forgive the men who raped me. I understand now that it was not my fault and that rape is a violent crime perpetrated by people with a soul sickness. Therefore, I pray for these men, wherever they are, that they may know the love, forgiveness, and peace of God that found me.

I blamed you for so long for not getting me the help that I needed to get through the rape when it happened; but perhaps if I had told you and Mom exactly what happened you would have. Maybe the truth is you couldn't have handled it then. Maybe it was all too much for any parent to know. I understand now that maybe it would have hurt you to know that you were not able to protect your little girl.

There is still so much I don't know. But one thing I do know is that I love you—always have and always will.

Dad, I guess you know that I never mailed this letter to you. I was holding it until the right time; but you died before my right time came. I always wanted to tell you what happened; but I never got the courage until now—and it's too late. Now that you are with God, perhaps He told you for me. Or perhaps you are reading it over my shoulder as I type the words that I scribbled on a steno pad a long time ago. I don't know.

Until we meet again, let us both rest easy and leave the profundities of life to the Author and Finisher of Life—God.

Moving forever forward,
Stanice—proud to be your daughter and namesake.

Writing that letter was hard, but if we do not expose our secrets to the light they will kill us slowly from the inside out. They are just too heavy for us to bear; but if we offer them up to God we will find the freedom that cannot be found in other things no matter how hard we seek. Sure, He knows them anyway, some of us say, but confession is good for the soul. It brings us out of the denial of what we've done or what's happened to us and allows us to move forever forward with our lives, in spite of—maybe even because of—what has happened.

Otherwise, we are in bondage to our past and cannot move forward. True joy eludes us and love cannot seep through the tightly webbed fortress that the secrets spin around our hearts and minds.

There are other benefits of exposing the secrets. We find that we are not alone—that we are not the only one. We find others who have done the same things or had the same things happen to them and they have made it through. We start to believe that if they can overcome, surely God being our helper, we can. If God forgives them, surely we can be forgiven. If they can forgive the most hideous of crimes perpetrated on them, surely, God being our enabler, we can forgive. We discover that God's love covers a multitude of sins and that darkness and light cannot coexist.

Perhaps God is urging you in your spirit to write someone a letter. Perhaps it's a letter to Him. Perhaps it's never to be mailed. Perhaps it is. That's between you and God. But write it like no one will ever see it. That way you won't worry about grammar but only what your heart has been yearning to express but knew of no safe way to do.

In my case, my letter wasn't meant to be mailed or it would have been; but I still believe that my dad read it. And my most fervent prayer is that God will use the letter to bless you, as it blessed me.

If there is no one whom you want to write a letter to, know that God is always ready to hear from you. Write a letter to our Heavenly Father. Invite Him into your life, confess how you have fallen short of His perfect way, tell Him your secrets, share with Him your pain, hopes, dreams, desires. Cast onto the written page all your worries and anxieties. Ask Him to make clear to you the path He has for you and His great love for you. Go on, tell God, "That woman Stanice told me that you are real and care about me and every detail of my life. So reveal yourself to me in a personal way. Show up for me like you show up for her."

Write, pour out your heart, cry over your letter like I did. Then, if it makes you feel safer, burn it. Watch the smoke spiral up like incense toward the Throne of Heaven. Come away from the experiences expecting and listening for God's response of unconditional, forgiving, and unchangeable love. Taste the glorious freedom of a personal and intimate relationship with God, the Maker of Heaven and Earth. And when the opportunity arises, and it will, share the letter exercise with someone else.

Dear Heavenly Father: Thank You for teaching us that our secrets die in the light of exposure and for setting us free from bondage to our past. We learn from our past and then move forward. We are grateful for the courage to speak and write the truth as we have come to know it so that You can make it perfect by adding Your unchanging Love. Grant us godly wisdom that takes us to further heights in life and in You than we could have ever imagined. Amen. So be it, in Jesus's name!

Reprinted by permission from Stanice Anderson, *I Say a Prayer for Me: One Woman's Life of Faith and Triumph,* (Walk Worthy Press/Warner Books), © 2002.

A High Price to Pay

LaVonn Neil

You were bought at a price; do not become slaves of men.

1 CORINTHIANS 7:23 NIV

I know all about the tremendous guilt and shame that are associated with an act of violence against another human being. I recall overhearing my great-grandmother telling my mother to pay close attention to how I reacted toward my stepfather, before their marriage. "Children are very perceptive and sensitive to people and situations in which they don't feel safe," my granny advised, which my mother totally dismissed as some sort of old wives' tale.

She should have listened.

Jonadab and Amnon devised a scheme in which Amnon could act on his lust for Tamar, his half sister. He knew his relationship to her and his position as King David's firstborn son, but that did not stop his infatuation with Tamar. The Bible describes Tamar as "a fair sister" and that she was a virgin and it was hard for him to get to her.

In reading over this passage, I look back over my life and see that I was in many ways like Tamar, a young beautiful child and untouched by man. The one who harmed me had to devise a plan crafty enough to prey on my innocence and vulnerability. He acted as any predator does, watching and studying his victim before making his move, taking note of habits, surroundings, families—especially if he is in it.

Not only did he know my family, he controlled it, convincing my mother and the authorities that I was being molested by a janitor at my elementary school. There were counseling sessions, police lineups . . . all based on accusations he had made.

I understand now that this was a way to divert the attention off of him and onto someone else. Many times I tried to tell my mother the truth. Each time, she dismissed me. Honestly, I don't believe that she ever heard me; she was so wrapped up in her own situation.

My mother had me at the tender age of fifteen and married the first man who asked for her hand. She often retracted things she'd said or done to keep from setting off his physical and emotional abuse. My sexual abuse continued for three years, usually when I was alone with him or getting ready for bed while my mother went on an errand.

I remember crying out to God in my room and asking, "Why me?" I was always taught, "Tell the truth and it will set you free," but each and every time I tried to tell the truth, I was punished severely. I couldn't understand what I could have possibly done in my young life to usher such deplorable punishment upon myself. I was waiting for God to step in and destroy the wicked and save the innocent. When all that I had learned in church and Sunday school lessons did not work for me, I lost hope.

I didn't know what to believe, who to trust, or if I could trust anyone. It was strongly embedded in me that I was not to discuss this matter with anyone. Ever. There would be times in which I would visit family members and they would strike up a conversation and I would say that I received a whipping for some mischievous behavior or for receiving a low grade, and once they discussed this with my mother, it was all over. I was never to discuss what went on in my household. So I withdrew from others and became very distant.

One Sunday evening at church a young man took the floor and talked openly about how important it was for parents with young children to listen to their kids' conversations. He was implying that as adults we get so caught up in our lives that we neglect to stay tuned in to what's on our children's minds. The whole time this young man was speaking, I felt that he was talking directly to me. I felt that he knew my secret and I swore that every time I lifted my head he was looking directly at me.

That night, I summoned enough courage and strength to tell my mother the truth one last time. I remember my mother standing in her room rolling her hair with those pink sponge rollers, and I asked her if we could talk for a second. Without missing a beat, she stopped mid-roll and looked my way. I told her the truth: that there was never anyone from my school molesting me, that it was, in fact, her husband.

My mother never questioned me. She did apologize and told me that I would never have to worry about him again. Then she said to go to bed and that she would take care of everything. You may be asking what made this time so different. Why was I determined to tell her now versus any other time? One reason was that I felt safe because my stepfather was incarcerated and there was no one but my mother, my baby brother, and myself. I always felt safe around my mother; it was my stepfather's presence that most frightened me.

Everything was going good in my world, until my stepfather was released from jail. We had no prior warning that he was being released—at least I didn't. My mother answered the door and a few minutes later he walked in my room and told me to go to bed. That was fine by me, because I knew that once my mother lit into him it was all over. Well, that never happened. My mother chose to stand by her man, and so the physical abuse continued.

I can say that he never touched me again sexually. What I did not know at the time was that my mother wrote him a nine-page letter in jail, and he knew that I had told her everything. He denied it. My mother's choice to stay with him made me feel unimportant and somehow responsible for the actions of her husband. My mother seemed to keep a closer eye on me than on her husband. She tightened the reins on her then eleven years young daughter rather than her grown husband.

I felt that I was the one being scrutinized and disciplined for maturing physically at an alarming rate. It wasn't until my stepfather decided to bring another woman into her home while my mother slept in the next room that she decided that enough was enough. It was because of the act of adultery that my mother packed all of her bags and our belongings and walked away from him for good. The physical and verbal abuse wasn't enough, molesting her child was not enough, but adultery was not tolerated!

In the years that followed, I built some resentment and hostility toward my mother. I was never rude and disrespectful toward her because she was my mother and I knew there were some lines that you just didn't cross with her and live. I became very reclusive and despondent. I sought the love and attention that I never received as a child in the hands of men who I felt cared for me and loved me . . . because they said so. I had no example of what love was. I grew up in a household where you had to fight to show your love, you had to fight to protect what was yours or lose it.

There's a huge misconception concerning sexual abuse and molestation in our country today. I remember when I first started speaking publicly about my sexual abuse, people felt that I was taking some sort of pride and fulfillment in "airing my dirty laundry," which is ridiculous to me because society's nonchalant attitude about and tolerance of sexual abuse has forced many victims to keep silent. We are oftentimes molested both by the predator and then by the system or the people who are supposed to protect us. Shame, guilt, and rejection then set in because everyone, including the predators, reverses the script onto the victim and portrays the sexual abuse as the result of "suggestive communication."

For years, I never discussed with anyone what took place with me. I remember sharing with a boyfriend my childhood trauma and he asked me why didn't I stand up to my stepfather. I asked him how I might've done that. I was eight and he was thirty. He then replied that there was something I could have done to stop him. Once again, I was made to feel as if I had done something to warrant his behavior. I vowed never to speak of it again to anyone. Thankfully, that was a vow I did not keep.

Some people question me about my openness concerning my testimony and I tell them that I have nothing to be ashamed of. I did nothing wrong at the age of eight to warrant or entice his perversity. They said I should just get over it. They were right, but it was easier said than done. The hardest part was telling the truth. My childhood and innocence were stolen from me by the person who was supposed to be protecting me. In sharing what happened to me, I give voice to so many other women who cannot speak.

I say sexual abuse is the world's silent epidemic. *Why didn't you tell someone?* This is the question that victims of sexual abuse are often asked. For myself, I had beaten myself up mentally by accepting guilt because I felt I should have told someone or answered truthfully when the detective asked me if it was my stepfather who was molesting me. The truth of the matter is, as a child, I was afraid of being taken from my mother and put in foster care or having both my parents locked up. I was afraid of truth's consequences. I had never known anyone who was being molested; this was not a normal topic for girls to discuss. But I had seen parents carted off to jail and children placed in foster care. I didn't want that for me or for my little brother.

Even when I told my mother the truth, I was sworn to secrecy. Silence adds to the feelings of resentment and shame because you internalize all that negativity and trauma, a breeding ground for emotional parasites such as anger, resentment, hatred, and rejection. Though families and communities want to protect themselves by keeping the victim quiet, she must somehow find her voice.

Amnon paid the ultimate price for his sin—death. For years I was angry and hurt, but I never wanted my stepfather to die for his actions. I have tried over the years to discuss with my mother why she didn't leave sooner, but she has chosen not to discuss this part of her life. Sometimes I think that hurt me even more than the things that happened to me. My bitterness caused me to hurt myself and people who wanted to be part of my life, people who told me the truth and wanted nothing but the best for me. I was blinded by my rage and destroying the good that was coming into my life. I didn't trust people because I thought love was something that only happened in fairy tales.

I reached a point in my life where I was tired of *existing* when I wanted to *live*. I remember getting down on my knees and praying to God that there had to be more to life than this. Surely I had a greater purpose than what had happened to me thus far. I was in my early twenties and I was trying to find myself and change the course of my life. I didn't have a clue as to how I was going to undertake such a tremendous feat but I knew that I must. After joining the army reserves and moving to Oklahoma to distance myself from my past, I quickly learned that you could travel the seven seas and change your entire appearance, but unless you change the enemy that resides within, you are destined to repeat that which you are running from.

I remember sitting at my kitchen table reading the emotional journal I'd started keeping. I burst into tears. Anger and blame were on every page. No one was safe, even the people I hardly knew. I remember hearing a small still voice whisper, "Forgive them!"

What?

"Forgive them."

Who?

"Forgive those whom you hold accountable!"

This was too much, but at the same time I knew that I had to do something. Forgiving them just didn't seem like it was the answer. Plus it was more easily said than done, because I had no clue how to go about forgiving the man who molested me and the woman who stood by him, forsaking her own flesh and blood!

Because of my love of writing, I sat down and wrote a letter to my mother. I said everything that I wanted to say to her. I asked her questions that I always wanted to ask her but never did. I sat down and wrote page after page; sometimes the tears would flow like a waterfall and other times, I would feel a burst of anger and tear a hole in the page by writing so intensely and vigorously. There were times when my emotions were too overwhelming and I would have to walk away from the journal; other times I would pick up the journal off the table and throw it clear across the room.

Little did I know that this was the beginning of my healing process. Every time a new question would come to mind, I wrote her a letter; every time I thought about the pain I felt as a result of her actions, I wrote her another letter. I didn't worry about penmanship, grammar, or the proper salutations, I simply wrote whatever I was feeling. I wrote tons of letters; some I wrote and kept, others I wrote and discarded.

I never mailed her a single one of my letters. That wasn't the point. I didn't write the letters for her to defend herself; I wrote the letters for myself. I wrote the letters because I was the one suffering and I was the only one with the grace of God that could heal the hurt and emotional havoc I was experiencing in my life.

After I started experiencing some breakthroughs, I was finally ready to take the big plunge and work on forgiving my stepfather. I followed the same process. I asked him questions that I always wanted to ask, I expressed my feelings without fear of the consequences, I told him what my life has been like for years due to the pain he caused. I screamed, I cried for myself, I cried for him. I cried for my mother and for every other child who has ever experienced being molested. I cried for the mothers who accused the daughters of inviting such an act. I cried for the daughters who had been abandoned by their mothers or their guardians. I cried for the generational curses of mothers who were molested as children and therefore didn't know how to protect their daughters because no one protected them. I cried until my tears had tears.

Once again, I never mailed the letters to him. It had been over a decade since I had spoken to or seen him. I didn't write the letter for him; it was for me. As a speaker, I travel the country speaking about sexual abuse and domestic violence and people often ask me how I could forgive a man who molested me. I reply that it's easy!

Many people have a misunderstanding about forgiveness. Forgiving someone who has wronged you has nothing to do with them and everything to do with you. It allows you to take back your power and stand firmly in it. It allows you to see and say to them that you are bigger than them and bigger than this experience. Forgiving someone who has wronged you in any way allows you to live and not just exist. Anger, resentment, vengeance eats away at you. It slowly kills and poisons your system. Your forgiveness is not a sign of weakness and vulnerability, it's a sign of strength and power.

Absalom had Amnon killed in retaliation for what he did to their sister, Tamar. Amnon's hatred and lies cost him his life! I took my life back the day I decided that my past did not and would not determine my future. I reached a point in my life where I was tired of giving this man power and control over me emotionally, spiritually, mentally, and physically.

If you have been violated in any way, whether by a member of your family, family friend, boyfriend, or complete stranger, then allow yourself the most precious gift you have—your life! Take your power back and reclaim your life.

After you forgive them, forgive yourself. Forgive yourself for believing that you did anything wrong. Forgive yourself for allowing others to make you feel as if you are unworthy. Forgive yourself for believing the lies that were told to you. Forgive yourself for believing that you aren't good enough.

Five years ago, I ran into my stepfather; I was in a hurry and not aware of his presence. When I heard someone speak to me, I looked up and there he was. I spoke to him genuinely and moved on. I was so amazed later that day as I kept reliving that particular moment, and I felt nothing but control and confidence. There was no hatred and no anger. It was at that very moment that I realized I had taken my power back and was living my life.

Father God, help us forgive those who have wronged us and by doing so free ourselves as well. Thank You for Your healing power. In Jesus's name, amen.

Beyond the Scars

Sharon Ewell Foster

The wife of a man from the company of the prophets cried out to Elisha, "Your servant my husband is dead, and you know that he revered the LORD. But now his creditor is coming to take my two boys as his slaves." Elisha replied to her, "How can I help you? Tell me, what do you have in your house?" "Your servant has nothing there at all," she said, "except a little oil."

2 KINGS 4:1–2 NIV

One day I went to an evening church service. The woman preaching told the story of a widow with two children who was having financial problems. She had my attention; I could relate. All the widow had was a vial of oil. The preacher told the story of a miracle that happened with the woman's vial of oil (2 Kings 4:1–7). Inside, I began to ask, what was my vial of oil—what did I have that I could use to care for my family and bless others? First, I thought, *Singing?* But nothing happened. Then it came to me: writing. That's what I should be doing, writing.

It took less than a day to talk myself out of writing. I was pretty efficient at crushing my own dreams. But it kept happening; different events kept pointing me toward writing. Then I would halt my crazy dream and focus on my career. The process continued—writing would poke up its head, then I would bury it. Until one day, toward the end of my leadership program year, I sat at my desk at Fort Meade fussing silently about my career. I was now employed as an instructor. I loved teaching, I loved speaking in front of people, but something was missing. I thought it was related to my career. Then it hit me. It felt like a concrete block literally hit my chest. I was supposed to be writing. I was supposed to be sharing the truth that I had learned so that I could help other people find the peace that I had found.

When I went home, I cried for two hours. I confessed in prayer that I was afraid and that I didn't think I was good enough, that I was not a trained novelist and didn't believe I could do it. But I committed to trying. What could trying hurt? I didn't have to buy anything or spend any money. I started with what I had. I promised that when I wrote I would tell the truth, even if it hurt.

I gave up an hour's sleep and rose each morning at five. Sitting on my living room couch, I wrote longhand on stenographer's pads. As I wrote, I began to feel better about myself. I felt more free.

One of the things I liked least about working was performance appraisals. I disliked them even more than filling out time sheets. Something about performance appraisals always left me feeling angry, depressed, and just not good enough.

It was that season and I was dreading it. I got my appraisal. It wasn't bad, but it wasn't glowing either. It didn't reflect all that I had done. I told my supervisor I wouldn't sign it.

I went back to my desk. It came to me that only I and my Creator could determine my value. It didn't matter what other people said. My happiness should not depend on them putting good labels on me. I was wonderful. In fact, around that time I found passages in the Bible that said that God sang songs to me and that He delighted in me. If that was true, what difference did a performance appraisal mean? If that was true, what difference did it even make what my family thought of me?

So I signed the appraisal. I apologized to my supervisor and told her that I was instead going to pray for her to get the promotion that she had been seeking. It changed our relationship. In fact, I believe that event radically changed my life.

But there was an even more difficult lesson to be learned about valuing myself. It was acknowledging first to myself and then to others the importance of my own dreams and interests. Maybe it was easier to ignore, bury, or ridicule my dreams myself than to risk someone else doing it to me.

Discipline is key to success, but so is self-respect. Successful people respect their own thoughts, ideas, and dreams. Some believe their dreams can put money in their pockets. Some believe their dreams can serve others. Some believe both.

It sounds so elementary. Of course I valued myself. That's what I thought, but my actions said otherwise. I made time to take my children wherever they needed to go—karate, swimming, play rehearsal, choir rehearsal, and to the mall. I talked to them about their dreams and what they could become. I encouraged every dream.

I didn't do the same for myself. I didn't have time to exercise. I didn't do anything fun for myself. Any flickering thought about any dream was quickly extinguished; the thought was foolish and I didn't have time. I would never have treated my children that way.

I had buried any ideas I had about writing so deeply that most times I didn't remember I ever had such a thought. I wasn't a good enough writer. I wasn't a good enough person. Who would want to hear what I had to say? There was no way to make any money writing. Who would want to pay for what I wrote? Many of my wounds were healing, but no one wants a girl with scars. I would have to be perfect for anyone to want me.

And that's how I felt about my writing: If it wasn't perfect, it wasn't worth showing. That's why I had so much difficulty writing: I felt it wouldn't be pretty enough.

Valuing and respecting yourself sounds simple until you begin trying to make time for yourself. It's simple until your thoughts and dreams come up against other priorities like grocery shopping, washing clothes, cooking dinner, staying at work past quitting time to finish a project that just *has* to be done, or getting the kids to track practice.

I committed myself and my time to everyone else, but not to me. Most of the time, I raised my children as a single parent. There was no other go-to person but me.

I wrote my first three chapters during those early mornings before my kids awoke so that I would have private time that would not interfere with my life with them.

Rising early is great, but as I needed more time to write, the answer was not to give up sleeping. I had to face making adjustments. I had to face that I couldn't do it all. It wasn't easy.

I was the person who could handle it all. I got things done at work, at church, for friends, and at home. I liked it that people relied on me. Even when I was drained there was a payoff: I found my value in the appreciation and approval of others, doing everything and never saying no. Their approval, though I didn't realize it at the time, meant a lot to me. I got it done and I was a good girl. I never said no or complained. I overdid it everywhere. Even at church I sang in the choir, taught Sunday school, served on the missionary board, cooked for special programs . . . I was doing and doing and doing, but I don't know that I was impacting anyone's life.

I substituted other people's approval for self-respect. Their approval took the place of any of my own dreams or ideas.

It wasn't an easy adjustment. People didn't just approve of me; I had made them addicted to me. Oh, how needed I was! They could count on me without thinking. They didn't even have to consider my needs or whether what they asked inconvenienced me or made me miserable, or even if it injured my health.

There was no point in getting angry at people for making too many demands on me. I did it to myself. What a martyr I was.

I was going to have to make the change if I wanted my life to change. I was going to have to find another way to tell people I loved them. I was going to have to risk that they would still love me if I disappointed them.

So I began negotiating with myself. What could I give up? It felt selfish to think of myself and my own needs. But it occurred to me that by the behavior I was modeling before them, I was teaching my children not to respect themselves. I was telling them to follow their dreams but contrarily showing them that I thought it was selfish to make room in my own life for myself, my needs, and my dreams. It was no less damaging than if, for instance, I had told them not to smoke while smoking myself.

Valuing oneself and selfishness are two very different things. I was not abandoning my children and the other people in my life. All of my time was not focused solely on me. I simply made time in my own life for me. I acknowledged that my children were extremely important, and my work, extended family, friends, and church were important too. (Church is separate from God to me. God is always with me and a partner in what I do. In fact, I feel it was His spirit encouraging me to love myself.) But what I added to this list was that I was also important.

I decided I would take back my lunch hours. I would no longer work for the federal government during lunch. I also decided that I would leave work on time; if it didn't get done, it would get done the next day. I stopped singing in the choir, which meant I freed up driving and rehearsal time, and I stopped attending every function.

My children and I talked about it. Everyone was excited—that is, until things changed.

At home, which was most heart wrenching, I demanded some time in the evenings alone to write. My children were my constant source of enjoyment and comfort, but I needed time now. While my children worked on homework upstairs or entertained each other, I wrote. If I'd been in another room watching television, I don't think it would have bothered anyone, but having me do something for me that was important for me (especially when all my attention had been devoted exclusively to my son and daughter) did not sit too well in the beginning.

My family adjusted. We all became more flexible. The change became worthwhile for them when they saw that I was happier and my happiness benefited them; I had more energy and I was more pleasant. Children love to see their parents smile, and I smiled much more.

They have learned to be more balanced and to live out their dreams. My daughter has earned her master's degree in history and my son is pursuing his master's degree in opera.

My job adjusted. (No one there knew why I was making the

changes. I only shared my secret with my two children.) They couldn't make me stay late. Besides, I still worked hard and they also benefited from a happier employee.

But it wasn't all easy. It wasn't all happily-ever-after.

I didn't tell my family of origin I was writing until after my first book had been published and won a major award. I lost friends. The attention and resources I shared with them was reduced. Some were happy for me, others felt abandoned. We had attended many pity parties together. We had railed against the ones who'd hurt us and blamed them for keeping us unhappy. Now I wasn't attending the parties. I was making changes.

My pastor was pretty ticked off with me. I think it felt like I was abandoning the church for this "little writing thing." My pastor was displeased and disapproved of my following my own dream. My children and I had to find another church.

All of it was part of setting boundaries and making room in my own life, room for blessings I believe God wanted to give me. Part of someone loving you is she or he respecting your hopes and dreams. Part of you loving yourself is doing the same.

Suddenly—or at least it seemed sudden—I began to believe good things about myself, and I had a dream. I dreamed a dream about the beauty of my scars; it challenged what I thought.

In the dream, I was beautiful: I was the right size, the right shape, all that. But I was covered from the top of my neck to below my ankles. My arms were covered to my wrists. I was smiling and wearing black, thinking that everything was fine. Then a voice spoke to me and told me not to hide—to show my arms, my legs, to show all of me. When I disrobed, I was ashamed because I was covered with scars. Then the voice told me that it was my scars that made me beautiful. The only way that others will know they can be healed is if you show your scars. I looked again, and my scars were in beautiful patterns.

No one wanted to marry a girl with scars, I had been taught. And that's how I felt about my writing: if it wasn't perfect, it wasn't worth showing. Just like my mother's vision for my legs, my vision for writing—if I ever did it—was a pretty one. I would write *Wuthering Heights:* "Oh, Heathcliff!" If I ever wrote, I would write about beautiful women and handsome men living beautiful lives in beautiful places, I had told myself. They would have passion and struggles . . . but definitely no scars. Their words would be pretty and grammatically correct. They wouldn't have roaches or bills; they wouldn't drive broken cars or wear stockings with runs; they wouldn't be raped or rejected.

Oh, and did I mention that they would be pretty? Because, everyone knows, the only women of any value are women with no scars. The only *writers* of value are writers with no scars.

The truth is that I am scarred. The scars tell the story of my life.

My scars allow me to have compassion for other wounded people—I know the pain; it is the mosaic of my healing and restoration. So, when I write, it is not Heathcliff on the moors in England. It is my own story: Armentia on the Trail of Tears in my book *Abraham's Well.* She survives the deaths of loved ones. She is rejected, she is raped, she is betrayed by her family and by society, but there is still beauty in her life. The process of being wounded is painful for Armentia, but she learns to allow herself to heal, she forgives, she overcomes. She learns, with all reason for hope being gone, to hope on. These are common themes in my books because my books are printed from my own scars.

Whether the books are humorous, historical, or about spiritual warfare, the words come from what I know; they are the impressions made from the scars on my body, on my heart, my soul, my mind, and my spirit.

My scars are beautiful because they are no longer wounds. I have moved through a healing process and I have been left with the symbols of my healing.

It isn't perfect, pretty writing about flawless women or men or children that has gotten me published; it is my willingness to honor my readers and my Creator by sharing the truth. My scars tell my readers that they can trust me, that what I say to them is authentic, not just a copy of what someone else wrote or told me. What I write comes from my belly. When I write about forgiveness, it is because I have felt the pain, and the beauty, of forgiving.

I still have some wounds that I must tend. I know what my mother did not—that sunlight and fresh air heal wounds. In order to be healed, the wounds have to be shown and acknowledged. There is balm for wounds, but you have to show the doctor so that you can get the medicine; you have to expose the wound so that the dressing can be applied.

When I awoke, I prayed, and I promised the Creator that if I wrote, I would show my scars.

It may sound unbelievable to some, but I have emerged from my journey a grateful woman. I have inherited great treasure from my family—intelligence, creativity, discipline, wisdom, and courage. It has been worth clearing away all the debris—anger, abuse, fear, depression—to get to it. Among my treasures are also those beautiful scars. And there is no doubt in my mind that I would not be the person I am if I had not accepted the quest to find the treasure buried within me, if I had not acknowledged that my scars in some way are a map for me. I don't think I was ready for good things in my life until I could see my scarred, imperfect life with all its complicated characters and details as good.

I am still working to believe in great things and to allow myself to dream fabulous dreams, and to believe those dreams are for me. I still have to remind myself that I am beautiful and that there is a great plan for my life and art. Sometimes I have to fight with myself for great things. Sometimes my children, who have learned to value themselves and me, have to encourage me to accept great things for myself. But I am on my way and I believe that if you find the courage to make the steps on your own heroine's journey, great things await you too.

Father God, thank You for allowing us to accept and move beyond the scars. Help us to value ourselves and our dreams. Give us the boldness and courage to make the journey You have planned for us. In Jesus's name, amen.

A New Name

Marilynn Griffith

He who has an ear, let him hear what the Spirit says to the churches. To him who overcomes, I will give some of the hidden manna. I will also give him a white stone with a new name written on it, known only to him who receives it.

REVELATION 2:17 NIV

One thing that often happens along the road to the Father's house, the path to healing from shame, is a name change. For some of my sistahs, like Claudia Mair, the new name came through new faith. For others, like Gail, new learning experiences crowned her as "Dr. Gail." Mine was a journey from Mary to Marilynn, a trip I'm still taking.

I was born Marilynn, but I never knew that was my name until I was nineteen and went to get a birth certificate to apply for a federal job. It went something like this:

The woman at Vital Statistics peered over her glasses at me. "We don't have anyone under Mary. All we have is Marilynn."

"That's impossible." I bit my lip, trying to make sense of what she'd said.

"It's true." She shrugged and grabbed another file.

I wrung my hands. "But I'm alive. I'm here."

She snorted. "Uh-huh. But who are you?"

She handed me the Marilynn birth certificate. I'd paid for it, after all. I tried to take it in. Someone else with my unusual last name? And born on the same day?

What in the world?

Like the flash of a camera, it came to me. After my mother had me, she developed an infection and had to go back into the hospital for a month. My grandmother and her affinity for double names—Donna Lee, Betty Lou, and so on—had renamed me "Mari Lynn." The truth gripped my mind like a vise.

I'd learned to write somebody else's name in kindergarten. It was on my high school diploma, even my social security card. I'm not sure how they got by with it, but everything in my life bore the wrong name. Still, it was the only me I knew.

I write under Marilynn because my writing is the part of me that is unknown, undiscovered, but destined from the beginning. Still, it is sometimes hard to think of myself as anything but "Mary" from round the way, though if you're not careful, I'll go Ngozi on you too.

I don't get too hung up on the name thing though. In the end I'll get a new name. A hidden manna name etched into a white stone.

My glory name.

So don't worry if folks confuse the new you with who you used to be. God knows who you are. He sees you. He loves you. And He's preparing a new name, one that your mother and father won't even know. A name forged in trials and triumph, a name made for His glory.

Besides, there are always more names along the road, like Mair, Claudia's chrismation name in the Orthodox church. She took Mary of Egypt as her patron saint. In the spirit, we now share a name. I love that. Recently, someone has taken to calling me Mari, a mixture of my new and old self. I like that too, but it's that secret name I'm waiting on.

So keep your head up and cherish your names, all of them. God knows who you really are.

Father God, thank You for knowing us so well that we'll have a name just for us. Help us to walk with You so closely that we'll move from identity crisis to Christ. In Jesus's name, amen.

Twelve Weeks of Truth —Week Six

Let love and faithfulness never leave you;
bind them around your neck,
write them on the tablet of your heart.

PROVERBS 3:3 NIV

DISCUSSION QUESTIONS

1. Stanice Anderson's "Confession Is Good for the Soul" allowed her to gain closure with her father even after he was dead. Have you ever written a letter to say something that you couldn't say in person? Think about someone in your life (living or dead) whom you need to express something to but for whatever reason you can't. Write them a letter, but don't send it. Shred it or discard it completely. Share with your group how this action made you feel.

2. Do you ever feel there is a part of you that no one except God understands? Write what your name would be if you had named yourself. Share with your sistahs. See who comes up with the most fitting new name!

3. Take a few minutes and write a blessing for yourself (about yourself!). Have those who want to read their blessings aloud.

Pray this prayer together:

Father God, thank You for sending sistahs to hold me with their words and remind me that the most important thing about scars isn't the wound but the healing! Help me to use my gifts and words to be Your healing hands. In Jesus's name, amen.

CHAPTER SEVEN

MY SISTAH'S KEEPER

So it came to pass, when they had brought them outside, that he said, "Escape for your life! Do not look behind you nor stay anywhere in the plain. Escape to the mountains, lest you be destroyed."

GENESIS 19:17 NKJV

We received many stories about women who had to escape. What struck us the most was how many women had difficulty leaving even though their lives were in danger. For some of us, perhaps God sent angels our way to help us get to safety. For some, He called us to be angels for others.

This chapter is special to me because more than once in my life, I've had to make a getaway. More than once, I've had to come to the aid of women who inspire me, women I love. As a young girl listening through apartment walls to the landing of blows and the hollow, hurtful silence that always followed, I purposed to never become a victim.

In my childish mind, things were simple: you decided what you would put up with and anything outside of that was unacceptable.

I was right . . . and altogether wrong. We all have places: broken, needy parts of us that will bend into another person's definition of love. Even when things twist and warp until we can hardly breathe, a woman, even a good-looking, educated, strong woman, can find herself in need of refuge. Though this might not have ever been your experience—and I pray that it never is—don't be so quick to judge the woman who didn't make the choices you think you would have made. One of the Laws of Thermodynamics says that everything that is at rest will stay at rest unless acted on by an external force. Some folks aren't moving because they can't. You may be the one God uses to get things going again, just by your smile, your listening ear, and your praying hands. She's still in there, she must might need some help.

Far Above Rubies

Marilynn Griffith

For her worth is far above rubies.

PROVERBS 31:10 NKJV

She was a gem. Almost a foot shorter than me, but so tall I felt small beside her. Her heart-shaped mouth uttered good things I'd never heard. Women things. When she placed her tiny hand in mine, anything was possible. People stared when they got on her bus, never having seen a driver who had to sit on a phone book. Her lips spoke nothing but faith. When she got off work as a bus driver, she drove her raggedy car with abandon, determined to change the world. I was just glad to ride shotgun. Especially that night.

My new roommates had made it to the apartment before me and taken all the keys, leaving a note on the door assuring me that they'd be home when I got back. They lied. Moriah and I knew it before we pulled up, but we didn't say it. It would have ruined the evening, an evening clear in her head but foggy in mine. We had three dollars between us. What kind of night could we make out of that? A forever night in the right hands, she said. And it would have been too.

We went to the movies first, with not even enough money to buy one of us a ticket. I tried to draw myself up, to shrink away. She strode tall, head high, waving for me to come on, giving me that look that said for me to trust her. I shrugged and met her at the counter.

"How are you?" she said to the man behind the cutout circle in the glass.

Surprised by the greeting, the older man with white kinky hair nodded, reaching for his head as if to tip his hat. Things stayed friendly like that until we got around to discussing the money for the tickets.

"We don't have any money, but the movie is almost over, and we don't need a seat. Can we just listen to the rest?"

I stared at the floor. I never could figure out where she came up with these things. I kept looking at the ground all the way down the hall as we followed the man into the theater. I don't remember what she told him after his initial refusal, but in the end, he was looking at the ground just like me. She had that effect on people.

We went to eat then, I think, with her buy-here-pay-here car hiccupping all the way. I took a sharp breath when she turned off the ignition at our destination. Would it start again?

"We'll get a jump from somebody." She patted the fender a few times. "I parked on a hill."

"Okey dokey," I said, trying not to sound doubtful. From the halfscowl she gave me, I knew I hadn't succeeded. What could I say? My idea of adventure was staying up late with a good book.

I don't remember what we ate. I can still hear her asking those men for a jump though, shaming them into helping us when they'd rather have passed us by. Years later, stranded on a road, I'd remember how she'd chosen the men she'd asked for help, wishing she'd used the same system on the men she'd let into her life.

As we'd silently prophesied, when we got to my apartment, no one was home. No key was waiting either. Though they'd all gone to the same place, no thought had been given to how I would get in. I'd learn later they were all too drunk to care about that black girl in the other room. It didn't matter. I was meant to go back to Moriah's house that night.

We limped into the drive near midnight. The house was dark and all her boarders sleeping. (Yes, she rented out her rental house. The girl was something.) We piled into her bed like a slumber party, mumbling about the group we were developing for sisters in the community. That night, I dreamed a sweet dream of sisterhood and tried to recall all the good verses from Miss Janie's Precept Bible study that I'd just left at home.

Questions tumbled through my shallow slumber. Would I walk with the Lord this semester as I had at home over the summer? Was the breakup with my boyfriend permanent? Would Moriah and I really change the world?

A knock at the door in the middle of the night brought an unwanted answer.

Exhausted by a day's sparkling, Moriah slept through the pounding noise. Still half-asleep, I rose and went to the door, never touching it.

"Yeah?" My voice sounded strangled as I tried to remember if one of Moriah's boarders was still out for the night. No, they'd been in bed before us. Who was this?

"Is Moriah there?" The male voice boomed from the other side of the door.

Was he kidding? What was it, like one in the morning? I became my mother for a minute. "She's sleeping. Sorry."

"Tell her it's Steve, from work. I really need to talk to her. It's important."

Without a word, I padded back to the room to share the visitor's ridiculous request. I slept like a log and would nap on you in a minute, but Moriah was even more serious about her rest. With a life like hers, she had to be.

Instead of laughing at me, she sat upright at the sound of his name. "Go back to sleep, Mary. It's that guy from work I told you about. The one who helped me get hired at the university after I stopped driving the bus."

I did remember. He had a degree, dressed nice, good job. He'd helped her out a few times when she'd come up short at the end of the month. Older than us, but he sounded like a decent guy. Still, I couldn't shake the feeling that she should see him tomorrow. An almost narcotic sleep came over me, though, as she climbed out of the bed and I climbed into it.

"Don't stay up late. I want to get home and try and make it to church. Maybe we can both go," I mumbled.

"Sure." She smiled and gave a little nod before turning off the light. Sleep took me then. Later, I would learn that at the same moment, Steve took her.

The sleep lifted from me as quickly as it had come. I awoke with a start. Where was I? Not home at my mom's. Not at my new apartment. Memories of the night before rushed to my mind. Moriah's. It was her rose-scented sheets I slept under. Her queen-size bed that I tossed in.

Alone.

The numbers on the alarm clock told me that over an hour had passed and my friend was somewhere other than her bed. I prayed and got to my feet.

"Moriah?" The volume of my voice surprised me. Though I was half-asleep, something felt very wrong.

After a pause, her voice, much calmer, much quieter than usual, came from the dining room. "I'm here, girl. We're going to go out for a minute to get something to eat."

Huh? Maybe if that was me it would have made sense, but Moriah didn't eat much more than a flea, and we'd had a late dinner. What was even open in her neighborhood this time of night? Again, my mother-mind spun. "This late? Are you sure?" I started for the door, put my hand on the knob.

Her calm voice changed octaves. "I'm sure! You stay in there and sleep, okay? Toss me my purse out here. We're taking my car."

My mind raced as I obeyed her. Driving the car that had put us down a few hours ago to go out for food she didn't usually want? Sleep pressed down on me again like a sedative, smothering my many questions, drowning my desire to go out there and give them both a piece of my mind. In the end, I don't remember quite what I said before the door shut, but I think it was something like, "Be safe."

She was not able to follow that advice.

When the phone rang again, I didn't reach for it. I reached for the bed behind me, the empty space where my friend should have been.

Ring.

I checked the clock. After three.

R—

"Hello?" I ripped the phone from the cradle. Before I'd just felt something might be wrong. Now I knew it.

"He—he . . ." It was my friend, moaning one word like a broken blues song.

Tears spilled down my face.

Lord, help me. What do I do? What do I say?

Be wise as a serpent. Gentle as a dove.

This was a job for my grandmother. So, in my heart, that's where I went. "What, baby? He what? What happened?"

"He hurt me!" She sang it again, only this time like a funeral dirge instead of a slow song. I sat down on the bed, not even aware that I had been standing.

What next? Smart. Be smart. "Is he still there? How did you get away?"

"The car stopped. I knew it would. He told me to wait or he'd kill me. Told me he wasn't going back to anybody's jail. Said he'd find me if I ran."

I closed my eyes. "Did he . . . ?"

"He did. Remember when you tossed me my purse? He'd already done it then. He had a knife to my throat. Said that if you came out, he'd kill us both. Kill us all."

Where were my jeans? My Bible? My hands were moving as fast as my mind. "Okay. Where are you?"

She broke down again, wailing in a way that stabbed straight into me. She was a warrior. My she-ro. And he'd hated her for it. "Some guys' house. They just come here to go to school. Eighteen. Nobody else would open their door for me."

"Let me speak to them."

They were church boys, I could tell. Raised right and scared to death. Taught to protect women and do right when they could. Wherever they are today, I pray blessings on their heads. "Can you bring her to me?" I asked them in a voice so steady it scared me.

They could. They did. I called the cops, telling the story as quickly and completely as I could.

"I feel so dirty. I want to take a shower," she said on the phone.

I froze. Wise as a serpent. "No shower. You'll wash off the evidence. Just come home, girl. I got you." I didn't have her. God did. And He had me too as I tried to think straight, sort things out. I'd managed to detach for moment, to pull away . . .

Until I saw her.

One eye sank back into her head while the other bulged, blinking at me. Her laughing mouth was swollen and bleeding. Bloody gashes crisscrossed the palms of her hands. She held herself at the waist, leaning over so I could see the missing clump of hair. If I hadn't known her, I wouldn't have recognized her. But I did know her, and so did those scared freshmen who had let her in their apartment. She was ruby. Onyx. Hyacinth. The king's daughter, thrust out by a thief.

"Will you stay and wait for the police?"

She shook her head.

I thought as much. I got in and told those sweet, smart boys to drive. I had the terrified drivers pull over at a gas station, where I put my last money in their tank and in the pay phone. The police were disappointed that we'd left the scene but said they'd meet us at the hospital.

They kept their promise. My friend was taken to a room while I recounted what I knew. After that, I stood alone in the hall. Crying. Praying. I called my Bible study leader Miss Janie back in Ohio from the pay phone. She had taught me how to pray . . . and how to dance. Though I didn't understand it myself, somehow she would understand. I don't remember what I told her. What I do recall is her steady, strong voice speaking God's word to me.

"God has not given you a spirit of fear, but of love, power, and a strong mind." Then came a prayer of covering, protection, and care. A prayer of light in darkness. As I listened, a man ran toward me.

"Are you Mary?" he asked.

I nodded, saying good-bye and following the hospital orderly. They wouldn't let me in before, but even in her pain, Moriah knew how to make her voice be heard.

"She needs you," he said in a tone that troubled me. Not "She wants you," but "She needs you." Only a man who worked on sexual abuse cases could distinguish the difference between want and need so quickly.

"Mar-eeeee!"

I heard her cry long before we got to the room. The floor faded beneath me as I ran to her, just in time to see an impatient doctor order a nurse to finish off what the monster had started.

"Please. Be gentle." She would never beg, even now. I knew that, so I begged for her.

In response, the nurse tugged out what seemed like a fistful of her pubic hair.

Moriah's nails dug into my skin. Our eyes locked. This was for the rape kit, to provide the evidence that would catch the man who did this, but at the time it just seemed crazy. At the same time, hysterical laughter poured from both our mouths. It wasn't funny. It was insane. But we'd done enough crying.

She went back up north after that. Back home, the one place she wasn't wanted, the place where no one saw her sparkle. The last time I saw her before the trial was when she came to my apartment to let me know she was in town. I answered the door with a pregnant belly and a busted lip. She looked worried for me. Sad for both of us. But when she left, she still called me Dr. Mary, the woman who'd help her change the world.

Even though it hurt, I managed a smile. She was going to be all right. He'd shattered the stone, but the sparkle was still there.

She was still something special.

Someone far above rubies.

Father God, thank You for protection, even in the midst of darkness. We praise You that no weapon formed against us shall prosper. Thank You for being the Light of the World when we need it most. In Jesus's name, amen.

A Place Prepared

Marilynn Griffith

*In my Father's house are many rooms; if it were not so,
I would have told you. I am going there to prepare a place for you.*

JOHN 14:2 NIV

A few years ago, I tripped over my book box and hit the ground hard, face first. My neck felt better after a few days, but I had a little extra lip on the side of my mouth for about a week. When things like this happen, I'm all the more thankful for my sturdy Nigerian nose and lips. My banged-up gums and scabs healed, but the stunned feeling I got when my face hit that plastic bin brought memories of another version of me, a sistah I thought might never recover, might never make it out.

A sistah who'd forgotten who she was and *whose* she was.

That day, that other time when pain blinded and surprised me, ended with a bottle of Guinness stout slammed into my mouth— by a man I'd thought I loved. A man I'd thought loved me. (I was just as crazy as him and had once kicked him while he was sleeping on the floor, just to be fair. But still . . .)

As the pain blasted across my face, I started to realize that our "relationship" hadn't meant as much to him as it had to me. At least not until someone else showed up and showed some interest. Then Mr. Nonchalant went loco, with his favorite drink in hand.

It took a beer bottle crashing into my face to sober me up to the reality that this wasn't going to end happily ever after. All I can remember saying is one thing.

"You hit me?"

It was a question more than a statement. Sure, we were living in sin, making a mess, but this? Naw. It was too, too much.

I just started walking. I wasn't sure where I was going, where I could go, but something told me that this was my rooftop, my precipice, and that the rest of my life dangled from this moment. Though something sorry and rotten in me was already trying to explain things away, the me that I'd shoved aside and stretched and strained, the Jesus in me, demanded to be heard.

"You've let him walk all over you. Under you. Your face was already on the bottom of his shoes. Now it's on his bottle of beer? Your name is Marilynn Ngozi Onyedika. Ngozi—"blessed." Onyedika—"leader of many." Child of God, keep walking. There's a place. A place prepared."

I didn't know Jesus spoke like Nikki Giovanni, but let me tell you, He said his piece (and his peace) that day. There was a place prepared, someone who cared for me and iced my face, who ignored the looks of his friends when they saw me. I tried to push him out of my mess ("a man is the last thing I need right now"), but he stuck by me.

Jesus stuck by me too.

Though I found my legs that day to walk away, many times my heart wandered back, wondering if I was worthy of real love (whatever that was). Each time, I knew it made no sense, that I was going to lose my good gifts, that my mama hadn't been wrong yet when she said somebody wasn't quite right for me, but it was hard just the same. Finally God showed me that my biggest fear then was leaving the craziness I knew for something unknown, something I feared might be worse. Little did I know that God had plans so infinite, so crazy good, that my only regret would be walking in disobedience for so long and missing out on God's best.

Wherever you are today, whatever you're afraid of, look at it and then look past it. Listen for the sound of a voice like many waters. Listen for the roar of redemption as God comes to wash you away to a new place, a place prepared. It's better than you can think.

Be safe and be ready. God's getting ready to pour out something amazing. Walk on, sistah. And don't forget your cup.

Father God, thank You for not only giving us a cup and filling it to overflowing, but for preparing a table, even in front of our enemies. You are a Good Shepherd, O God. Help us to hear Your voice. In Jesus's name, amen.

The Naked Pregnant Lady in the Yard

Claudia Mair Burney

For the hurt of the daughter of my people I am hurt.

JEREMIAH 8:21 NKJV

I was talking with my husband one morning. We were watching one of the morning talk shows drone on. This one was about abused women; the poor souls seem to be everywhere in the media these days.

It was not uncommon then for me to hurl accusations at the television, hissing and booing my contempt for batterers at my safe little television. I couldn't think too hard on the mournful ghost faces of the women—their bowed backs, their dead eyes shining with tears.

I was one of those women—a person who let such horrible things happen to her that most times I can't bear to think of them now. But there are times, like when I was watching that show or, later, discussing it with a friend, that the memories come, sometimes with startling clarity.

I am twenty-seven years old. A mother of one son. I am still pretty, if you can look beyond the haggard appearance that being constantly physically, psychologically, and sexually abused imposes on your body.

We'd argued, and he had grown fond of a particularly cruel indignation. He would force me to strip and toss me out of the house naked. I remember the quiet resignation and dead affect when unbuttoning my dress and stepping out of my underwear. My body was ripe with his child, the belly round as a peach, the hips flaring out wide in expectation. I should have been his joy and his reward, but I was the object of his hate, a constant reminder that life did not go his way, and he was forced to keep me for appearance's sake.

He'd grab me by the arm and shove me out the door, slamming it shut and bolting the locks. I would stand there, bewildered, almost high, blocking out the reality so that I could endure it. I never felt the horror of it while it was happening. I simply asked myself, *What do I do now?*

I wandered in this deadening daze across the street, glad that no cars were coming by. It is very difficult to cover yourself with bony arms and small, girlish hands when you weigh all of 110 pounds fully pregnant. A man came out of his house shocked to find me in his yard.

He was tall and young and handsome, brown and sun loved, and when he spoke, I heard his island accent. He came to me, with his arms stretched out like he wanted to cover me, but he didn't. It was as if he was afraid to touch me. Like I would break. Like I would shatter in his hands.

He spoke tenderly with his soft, lilting voice, but his questions were rapid-fire. What has happened? Who did this to you? And I answered him with the truth. I saw the disbelief and horror in his eyes. He could not comprehend the kind of cruelty that throws a pregnant young woman naked into the streets. I could not either, but for a moment, I was outside of myself. That wasn't me naked and pregnant, explaining to a kind stranger. He told me he would call the police, and I begged him not to, fearing the man I lived with would kill me if I ever got the law involved. I was in Maryland, far from home and people who loved me, and he had my son in the house.

The man went inside and came out with a bathrobe to cover me. He told me he called the police. You know what? I can't remember what happened after that. I don't remember if I ever saw the police, or when I went home, or if I ever returned the bathrobe. It's gone. The rest of that story hides in some dark corner in my mind and refuses to reveal itself to me.

These memories, they come like a distant discordant tune. Strange music that I don't understand. I hear the melody but don't remember the name of the song. I don't hear it often, not even when I watch talk shows. Somewhere she, that naked girl, stopped being me. Somewhere, Jesus came with outstretched arms . . . and He covered me.

I wonder if that man prayed for me. I think he did. I sure hope so. I also hope that if you ever find a naked pregnant woman in your yard, you'll cover her. Please, I beg you, cover her. Call the police, pray for her.

Remember her, many years later, when she is older and loved, and the mother of seven. Because sometimes, when she least expects it, she will find herself unable to stop crying while she types on her laptop computer, mourning the woman she was, the woman she had no strength to mourn back then. Think of this woman, too, and say another prayer for her, for she is all around you. Maybe she's even still in you. If so, go toward the everlasting arms of Christ, who covers us all.

Father God, thank You for covering us when we have no way to do so. We come now, under Your mighty wings, for rest and refuge. May nothing separate us from Your love. In Jesus's name, amen.

Twelve Weeks of Truth —Week Seven

Bear one another's burdens, and so fulfill the law of Christ.
GALATIANS 6:2 NKJV

DISCUSSION QUESTIONS

1. It's easy to discuss someone's burdens, but it's much more difficult to bear them. Sometimes we are blessed with safety so that we can be a place of refuge for someone else. However, we must use wisdom when dealing with sistahs in trouble, careful to keep everyone safe. Can you think of a time when you had to play sistah's keeper to a friend in need?

2. In Claudia Mair Burney's "The Naked Pregnant Lady in the Yard," did you feel her nakedness as your own? Have you ever felt numb to what was happening to you?

3. One of the best things we can do for a woman in danger is listen to her. Sometimes she will take our advice. Sometimes she will go back into danger. We must love, listen, and keep ourselves and our families safe while leaving an open door for this woman to walk through when she is ready. Has anyone ever just listened to you? How did that make you feel?

Pray this prayer together:

Father God, help me to speak gently to my mother, sisters, coworkers, and friends, even when they talk to me crazy. Help me remember that shame can bring a sistah down. Use my hands to lift someone up. Give me ears to hear and a heart to listen. In Jesus's name, amen.

CHAPTER EIGHT

HER ROBE, ROYAL NO MORE

Now she had on a long-sleeved garment; for in this manner the virgin daughters of the king dressed themselves in robes. Then his attendant took her out and locked the door behind her.

2 SAMUEL 13:18 NASB

Though Amnon took Tamar's virginity, it wasn't the only loss. The care with which Tamar kneaded Amnon's cakes, her identity as a daughter of King David, and her sense of belonging in the palace—all these were lost too. In this chapter, women tell of the emotional and mental costs of shame . . . and how Christ redeemed the remnants of their self-esteem into a new garment.

Scars

Claudia Mair Burney

"If you'll hold on to me for dear life," says God, "I'll get you out of any trouble. I'll give you the best of care if you'll only get to know and trust me. Call me and I'll answer, be at your side in bad times; I'll rescue you, then throw you a party. I'll give you a long life, give you a long drink of salvation!"

<small>PSALMS 91:14–16 MSG</small>

I have scars on my wrists. On the left wrist, the line is jagged and unsure. I cut that one first, probably because I'm right-handed. I wasn't committed to the idea of killing myself just yet. By the time I got to my right wrist, it was a little easier. That one is a clean, determined line, made once the shock of seeing the red beads of blood seep through my open flesh had died down.

The scars are very faint now, and I don't think about them much. Though there are occasions when I'm handing money to a cashier or something to a colleague at work, and I find myself hoping that they don't notice. No one has ever asked me about them though. I guess it would be impolite to do so.

I remember that awful day, and the startling ordinariness of it. The sun rose, just as expected. I got up, started my day, went to work, just like today, the exception being I go to work at night now and leave when the sun rises.

And then something went wrong, just like today. It was work related. Like today. I felt sad and hopeless, like today. I had Jesus, like today. So why am I not dragging razor blades across my wrists?

I don't know. Maybe because like that day, I really don't want to die. You gotta admit, slicing your wrists the wrong way is a pretty punk attempt at ending your life. Maybe I've grown up since then. Or maybe because even though I'm about to be fired, and I'm worried about how I'll feed my kids and keep a roof over our heads, I know somehow that Jesus will help. He'll have pity on me, because I don't have anything left but Him. And I'm not above the embarrassment of throwing myself, hard, on His mercy.

Many people would find the idea of God pitying them about as distasteful as women confessing their suicide attempts. I like God's pity. I find it comforting. Besides, I'm still here. There are no razor blades in my hands, which I stopped typing with to lift toward heaven in thanksgiving, scars and all. I've discovered something that young me was still struggling to discover. Jesus loves me. He has pity. He won't mind being my hiding place on days like today when I've taken to my bed and am hiding like a fugitive.

And here you are with me. Young me didn't have a community of people to love her, to listen, to talk. No one to send her prayers, quote the Word, and send her e-mails that let her know that she wasn't alone. Young me didn't have sistahs in the faith, holding her up, pulling her through.

Today I know that Jesus didn't mean for me to try to make it alone. I don't have to hurt myself, because He is here. My sistahs are here. And you are here too. Thanks for coming to see my scars. There won't be any new ones.

I'll see you at the party. I'll be at the bar, drunk with the wine of His salvation.

Father God, thank You for inviting us to the party every day. Thank You for the healing of scars and the reminder that though bad days come, You are always there. Come into our minds and heal our hurts there too. In Jesus's name, amen.

Perfection

Dr. Gail M. Hayes

To all perfection I see a limit; but your commands are boundless.
PSALM 119:96 NIV

"It's perfect," I whispered as I placed the silky nightgown on my freshly made-up bed.

The blue flowers on the nightgown's fabric reminded me of a brilliant summer sky. The pink reminded me of my favorite shade of lipstick, intense and hot. The yellow flowers touched the blue and pink just enough to make a turbulent rainbow blend. It was me—intense, depressed, beautiful, and angry.

"Everything is ready," I said, looking in the mirror just above my bed and gently patting my hair, usually worn in a thick Afro, but now formed into soft curls. Gazing at my reflection was my pastime. I knew that I had looks because I always seemed to cause a stir among men wherever I went. Unlike the men I'd met, the mirror did not lie. But that's another story.

Could it have been something else other than my looks that caused the stir? I dared not think otherwise. I gripped and wallowed in what I thought was my only means of salvation, my suitcases filled with lotions, potions, powders, lipsticks, and nail polishes. Making sure I looked good kept me sane. I had to keep it together. But after today, it wouldn't matter.

"I've got my nightgown, my hair done, and my bed made. My favorite white slippers with pink roses are by the bed. Now all I have to do is get dressed and . . . get the pills."

Pills? Yes, pills. I knew that the Tylenol was the only thing we had in the house. Mama always kept them in the kitchen. I quietly opened the cabinet, hoping the familiar squeak of the door would not send out its alarm.

I touched the cabinet with my fingertips like a classical guitarist stroking the strings of his precious instrument. I had to be gentle. I had to be quiet. I had to remain undiscovered.

I was successful at opening the cabinet door. The squeak decided to stay silent that day. Things were going just the way that I planned them, smooth, easy, and silent. This was my chosen time. With eight people in the house, there would not be another opportunity that offered such privacy. As I searched for the oversized bottle, I knocked over several smaller bottles before I found my prize, the 250-count bottle, filled to the brim with the chunky, chalky pills.

"Who's in the cabinet?" Mama called from the back of the house.

"Oh, it's just me, Mama." I answered, angered by my clumsiness and hoping she would not ask why.

"Oh, okay. Just checking," she replied. "Just wanted to make sure it wasn't one of your brothers. You know how your brothers are. They are always getting into things without asking a soul for help."

"Yeah, Mama. You are so right. But they wouldn't get away with much today. I'm on my job."

I heard the muffled sound of my parents' voices easing back into conversation. The tension filled the air with the dense fog of anger.

Mama had just received a call that she and Daddy needed to go and get my sister. My sister and Daddy had had an intense argument just a few weeks before and she'd left home. She'd threatened to leave before but never made good on her threat. This time, she left and did not return.

My sister was skilled at using systems so she would survive. She left home and ended up at the Salvation Army as the cook. She would call and let the phone ring once, letting me know to pick it up the next time it rang. She stayed there for a few weeks and then ended up in a rehabilitation center. Something went wrong and the staff called my parents and requested that they come and pick up my sister. They were in a heated discussion about whether or not to respond to the call.

This was the perfect time for me to complete my mission. They were distracted and could not interfere.

Yes, tonight things were going to be fine. Things were going to okay. Tonight, as I forced the bitter-tasting, bulky pills down my young throat, I knew that things were destined to be . . . perfect.

And yet, mercy said no to my perfect plans. Instead, God chose to spare my life and allow me to be used for the perfecting of the saints. Though shame may cause you to lay out your burial clothes, know that God still sees you in the royal robes given when you first believed. Be comforted, daughter of the King. God will perfect all that concerns you.

Father God, thank You for perfecting everything in Your time. Thanks for the new outfit too. This robe is beautiful! In Jesus's name, amen.

When I Think I'm Unlovable

Robin R. Wise

For I am convinced that neither death nor life, neither angels nor demons, neither the present nor the future, nor any powers, neither height nor depth, nor anything else in all creation, will be able to separate us from the love of God that is in Christ Jesus our Lord.

ROMANS 8:38–39 NIV

Even though it was February, this particular day felt like the coldest day of the year. As my eyes scanned an e-mail, Devastation had begun its work, slowly consuming me. The words "I'm sorry it didn't work out" grew bigger and bigger. My heart seemed to stop beating. It felt like it had exploded into a trillion tiny pieces with no matching ends.

My body felt like it was on fire. What was happening to me? Had a ton of bricks fallen on me and knocked my guts out? Now my heart was beating so fast that I thought it would literally jump out of my chest—*leaving yet another empty hole*. At that very moment, my lungs felt like they were collapsing. Frantically I started gasping for air. My legs weakened to the point that they felt like Jell-O. My world was falling apart. My lips were moving but no sound could be heard—*a silent scream*. No tears were shed, only the foul-tasting groans of Agony saturating my mouth, which crept from the bottomless depths of my soul.

Rejected again! I had to get away, but where could I go? Where could I run? Where on earth could I hide without Pain following me? I ended up driving in an endless circle trying to escape the truth of reality.

Seconds became minutes. Minutes became hours. Hours became days. Days became weeks. Weeks became months, as I sat imprisoned within the walls of Disappointment that were cemented in time by Hopelessness; hidden under a blanket of Fear and cowardly peeking through life's windows that Discouragement had so vividly painted in gloom. I wanted to die!

With each passing moment that ticked away, my mind began to be taunted by Shame and Humiliation, soiled with Betrayal and Confusion that kept wrapping me tighter and tighter, drenching me heavily in Insignificance. My bleeding heart mumbled, "Lord, I really thought he was the one."

(Ladies, we all know the drill . . .) *But, Lord, he goes to church and he seems to love You. He is my knight in shining armor. He is everything I ever dreamed of and most of all . . . I love him. Father, I did pray for guidance because after all I am getting older and no one else has really shown any interest in me. But did I neglect to listen to Your voice because I wanted who I wanted?*

As the hot tears formed to stream down my cold, numb cheeks, I soon knew that my eyes would tire from the heavy saturation of Weariness and my feeble body would become limp and motionless as my late-night visitors anxiously prepared to enter my bedroom to console me in my bed of Woe.

I awoke and walked around in a daze for months, building a fortress of Bitterness, pretending to be happy. Faking a smile here and there. Holding meaningless conversations . . . just wishing the other person would soon shut up so I could escape back to Lodebar, my secret isolated refuge—a place of barrenness, brokenness, and no communication—to bathe in my tub of bubbling Misery.

Emotionally and spiritually drained, I looked up toward heaven and God spoke to my spirit and said, "Robin, My daughter, I love you in spite of . . ."

"How could you love someone like me?" I asked. "Just look at me! A wretched mess all covered with Sin and Shame."

"In spite of . . . ," He repeated as He gently extended His hands of Mercy and Grace toward my broken, feeble body. He began gathering all my pieces, not to patch me, but to remold, reshape, restore, and revive a whole new me.

"Father, how could you love an unfaithful wretch like me? I have been unstable and inconsistent in my walk with You. I keep making stupid decisions and getting soul-tied with the wrong man. I have not completely trusted You to handle every area of my life. I have been angry and often blamed You when things went wrong."

"In spite of . . . ," He repeated as He continued to draw closer to me.

Now my tears were falling like big drops of rain. "Father, I am a murderer. I had an abortion that robbed my child of the opportunity to walk, play, cry, laugh, jump, be hugged, and be loved. I mistreated the son You gave me because he was diagnosed with ADD and didn't function as 'normally' as the other kids, and since I truly didn't understand his disability or the struggles he faced, my ignorance often led to emotional, physical, mental, and verbal abuse toward him.

"I was involved in adulterous relationships and allowed the wrong men to touch me in the wrong places. I endured the wrong relationships, which often consisted of the same mental, physical, emotional, and verbal abuse my son endured from me because I thought it was . . . love. How on earth could you love such a dead dog as me?"

"Robin, my daughter, I love you in spite of . . ."

I tried to hide my nakedness by covering my face from the shame. His Word, which I had hidden in my heart, became living and active to me; *again* He turned to me and heard my cry. He lifted me out of my slimy pit—out of the mud and mire. He set my feet upon a rock and established my steps. He became my refuge, my strength, my strong tower, and my present help in time of trouble. "I am He who sustains you; I have made you and I will carry and rescue you."

Because of His Mercy and Grace, He did not cast me from His presence nor take His Holy Spirit from me. He did not reject my prayers; instead He removed my sackcloth of mourning and began to wash me in His blood. He restored me, healed my wounds, covered my scars, and spoke life into my barren places *again*. Then He clothed me in His majesty and placed His robe of Righteousness upon me. He placed a brand new song in my mouth and displayed me in Garments of Praise.

He summoned me by name and beckoned for me to draw

closer into His outstretched arms. He invited me to partake of the feast He had prepared just for me. He reassured me that He loved me "in spite of . . ."

The first step was not an easy one. I struggled with Familiarity and tried to keep my balance, while Imperfection and Condemnation suddenly appeared to greet me and to remind me of all my faults and flaws. With one foot in front of the other, I was determined to come out of Lodebar—a land of aborted dreams, suffocated visions, and bitter hopes—to draw closer to my Father.

Even though the walk seemed dark, I was quickly reminded that when I walk through the Valley of the Shadow of Death, I will fear no evil, for His rod and staff comfort me. When I am afraid, I will trust in Him. No weapon forged against me shall prosper. He commands His angels concerning me to guard me in all my ways. What He has said, He will bring about. What He has planned, that He will do.

My old enemies, along with a few new ones, Disgrace and Torment, sneered and shouted accusations of my past against me and unpleasantly remarked, "Who does she think she is and where does she think she is going?" At that moment, Confidence and Boldness were the echoes of each step I made . . . as I continued to draw closer to my Father's presence to abide in love and peace.

In the presence of my enemies (Disappointment, Hurt, Shame) He prepared an elaborate table arrayed with the finest china just for me. As we supped, He became my portion, which caused my cup to overflow. He told me that I have been redeemed, forgiven, healed, delivered, and set free for His glory. He rebuked my enemies and called me to rest in the green pastures that lay beside the quiet streams.

When I allowed my Father to visit me in the midnight hour, He repeatedly began to administer a Well of Worth to me. He spoke into my spirit and showed that I am beautiful, I am significant, and all my imperfections were hidden in Him. He told me I am the apple of His eye, an intelligent divine original, and I am uniquely refined and shaped in my own destiny—a splendor of

His display. He told me I am His choicest vine because He loved Him some Robin Rene Wise, and I am accepted in the Beloved (and men led me to think I am unlovable).

Now, as I close my eyes, falling *again* into another deep, deep, deep sleep smiling confidently, I know that no one on earth could love and adore me like my Father because I am His precious and valuable jewel looking forward to the dawning of each new day . . . loving and celebrating the whole new me. *I will not die but live and proclaim what the Lord has done.*

Father God, we thank You for what You have done. We celebrate our new lives by proclaiming that we will use our lives as a testimony to Your power and grace. Though sometimes we feel unlovable, we praise You for never waning in Your desire for us. In Jesus's name, amen.

Uncovering Love

Delores M. Jones, MSW

*But be ye doers of the word, and not hearers only, deceiving your
own selves. For if any be a hearer of the word, and not a doer,
he is like unto a man beholding his natural face in a glass:
For he beholdeth himself, and goeth his way,
and straightway forgetteth what manner of man he was.
But whoso looketh into the perfect law of liberty, and continueth
therein, he being not a forgetful hearer, but a doer of the work,
this man shall be blessed in his deed.*

JAMES 1:22–25 KJV

There's power in being able to choose, even if, in the end, you
have to choose yourself. As I sought to discover my worth after
suffering domestic violence, I knew that God had admonished
me to think on "whatsoever is true, honest, just, pure, lovely, of
a good report, virtuous, and worthy of praise." I was also to put
into practice the things that I have learned and received and heard
and seen in Him. In all this, I was to trust that the God of peace
would be with me (Philippians 4:8–9).

Eventually I asked myself, "Where does a little girl learn to
love? Who teaches her how to recognize the attributes of love,
the actions of love, and the contradictions of love?" Mama and
Daddy should do it. You know, show me how to love.

But before they could teach me, both were gone. My mother
died at twenty-one after someone injected her with an overdose of
heroin that stopped her heart. She was gone. Murdered. Her love
for me lingered in my heart and soul, but the lessons about love
were interrupted, cut short when I was just five years old.

My father was simply in love with his dream of making it big
in Hollywood, and so he moved to California, where good times
and drugs became his main thing. The lesson I learned was "Never
love a man who reminds you of your father."

I suppose my life was not completely void of love. I experienced something I call "strange love." It seemed strange to me that the woman who raised me, could utter the words *I love you* and then turn around and call me a female dog. She would tell me how beautiful I was and encourage me to do my best in school because I was going to be somebody, but when her anger flared up, I once again became the dog. Interestingly enough, this woman whom I began calling Mama out of respect and appreciation for her willingness to keep me and my brothers out of the foster care system, also introduced me to God. A strange love indeed.

In trying to work through my grandmother's emotional roller coaster of love and name-calling, I would remind myself of scriptures about honoring your mother and father so your days will be long on the earth, verses that I had learned in Sunday school. At times they kept me from acting out, but they never stopped the pain or damage done to my self-esteem and ideas about love. My foggy understanding about love clouded even more when my male babysitter decided I was special and deserved extra attention from him, especially when my other brothers and sister were outside playing.

Frank was a kind man and often the brunt of many jokes from young and older people. He usually shook his head and laughed about their hurtful antics. He never complained. He taught me about what I have come to know as "undercover love." I knew the way he placed me on top of him was not right, but I had decided that I loved him as my babysitter and I did not want anyone to hurt him anymore. If I didn't tell, no one would know and he would not be hurt, especially by "Mama." I recall a time when she became very upset with him for eating the neck bones out of the pot of beans. She caught him doing it, and that day she taught him a lesson.

While he sat on a chair in another room, trying to flee her cursing, she stood over him with the pot of beans and neck bones in her hands. I watched as she poured the beans and neck bones over the top of Frank's head. As the food dripped down his head and face, he didn't say anything. He got up and walked away. He did the same thing the day she lit a cigarette and burned him. My sister had accidentally bumped into his cigarette as we played outside that day. It was an accident, but Mama did not believe him. She decided to teach him yet another lesson.

I pitied Frank and never wanted anyone to hurt him. I endured his touching, rubbing, and molestation for a few years for fear that if I told, someone, maybe Mama, would kill him.

The day I cried out to God about my choices about love in my life, He brought back that experience to the forefront of my memory. I was now thirty-six years old and alone.

As I cried and cried I realized that once again I had become that little girl who refused to tell anyone that someone was hurting her, because of what I called love. In this relationship and others, I had recognized the patterns early on, but once I said "I love you," I had a tendency to ignore the obvious and sweep the issues under the rug.

One day a friend shared with me that I was the common denominator in the troubling, violent relationships I found myself in. At that moment it became clear that I needed to pay attention to the patterns in my own behaviors that helped perpetuate the destructive relationships that I allowed or attracted into my life. Coming to terms with the truth about love and my part in it meant I had to embrace and follow through with what I had come to learn as truth.

The truth is, God is love. Love is an openly beautiful thing that promotes the best in a person emotionally, mentally, physically, and spiritually.

Love respects boundaries. An understanding of love also requires responsibility. I am responsible for loving me even if no one else does. Failure to do so is insanity. It's not sacrifice, compassion, or consideration on my part when I tolerate hurt that someone else calls love. Love is not about covering up a wound. Love is a wonderful thing.

Father God, thank You for showing us what real love is. Help us to be patient and kind to ourselves and to others. Show us each day what real love is. It's good to uncover true love at last! In Jesus's name, amen.

Deliverance

Shelette Carlisle

My whole world is starting to fall apart.
All the people in it seem to have no heart.
The only friend that I really had left me a long time ago,
which made me sad.
I was depressed for quite some time.
Until one day I saw this sign.
This sign let me know that I needed to go on.
It also let me know that I wasn't alone.
However, from that point on, I began to block people out.
I built up a wall to guard my heart, my mind,
my body and my soul.
That's why people say that in place of my heart there's nothing
but an empty hole.
But through experience, there are many lessons that I learned.
I've learned that you have to respect yourself in order to
get the respect of others and that respect has to be earned.
I've learned that you have to love yourself
before somebody can love you.
I've also learned that you can't depend
on other people to make you happy.
You can only depend on yourself.
I've learned to never give up,
no matter what kind of hardships you are enduring.
And if you never give up, you'll have deliverance
from situations that are alluring.
But my ultimate deliverance came by realizing
that only through the grace of God
will you make it through.
And in the end, you'll realize that
He's the only real friend you knew.

Twelve Weeks of Truth —Week Eight

Therefore, as God's chosen people, holy and dearly loved, clothe yourselves with compassion, kindness, humility, gentleness and patience. Bear with each other and forgive whatever grievances you may have against one another. Forgive as the Lord forgave you. And over all these virtues put on love, which binds them all together in perfect unity.

COLOSSIANS 3:12–14 NIV

DISCUSSION QUESTIONS

1. Perhaps, like the women in this book, something happened in your life that uncovered you emotionally, physically, or spiritually. Well, God has a new outfit for you: compassion, kindness, humility, gentleness, and patience. It may be a tight fit at first, but as you listen and love one another it will become easier. This week did you uncover love in one of these stories? Would you have made the same decisions that these women made?

2. Do you think that you are lovable? Write down ten things that you love about yourself. Repeat this exercise and make a list about each person in the group. Exchange lists and compare with your own. Are you surprised by any of the answers?

3. While we are clothed with kindness and humility, we cannot let shame fix on our faces like a mask again. Secrets are hard to tell, but they are also hard to keep. Whenever you feel like you have to lie to your family and friends, something is probably wrong. Name some red flags in

relationships that you have discovered. What do you do when one of these "flags" flies up on a date or early in a relationship?

4. In "Uncovering Love," the same person who taught Delores about Christ also exhibited abusive behavior. Has this been your experience? Discuss ways that we as women can overcome abuse without becoming abusers.

Father God, I thank you for blessing me with a new outfit of kindness and compassion. Have mercy on me as I try to be better, both to my friends and to myself. Help us to remember how much you love us, even when we don't feel it. In Jesus's name, amen.

CHAPTER NINE

MY REARGUARD

Then your light will break forth like the dawn, and your healing will quickly appear; then your righteousness will go before you, and the glory of the LORD will be your rear guard.

ISAIAH 58:8 NIV

There isn't much worse than thinking you're looking good only to realize things are hanging out in all the wrong places. Sometimes though, it can't be helped. You hurt too bad to hold your gown closed. Your heart is too broken to pull your pants up. I've had days like that—days that require the grace of a good God, the love a good man, and the wardrobe of kindness from some good friends.

When they came to take my baby away and my fourteen-year-old fingers jerked across the documents, I felt like that. Naked. Raped. Betrayed. But what could I do? The lawyer, my mother, the nuns . . . they'd made their points clear. I had nothing. Was nothing. And nobody was going to pick up my slack. If I had any notion of what love was (they obviously doubted it), I would do the right thing. Too bad Spike hadn't made the movie then.

So I lay there, bleeding, in such a horror of pain, pain that didn't seem possible. A head-to-toe ache from the Pitocin-epidural war of my induction. It was my birthday. They brought me a cake with no candles and fake smiles. I stared right through them. It wasn't the gift I needed.

What I needed was down the hall, crying in the hands of strangers. And so I went, forcing one quaking leg in front of the other, gripping the walls with trembling hands, my hair a crazed halo of Jheri curl.

"Look at that child. Her behind all hanging out," one of the cleaning ladies whispered to another. They didn't try to cover me either. I wouldn't meet the kind of women who would cover me until much later. I could feel their heads nodding behind me, but I didn't stop to cover myself. There was no time. I would faint soon.

I made it to the glass. There she was, so small, so sweet. Like an old woman she looked up at me, through me, like those silly birthday people had. "I'll be all right," her eyes seemed to say. "You won't." I swallowed before I hit the ground, knowing she was right.

Now, many children and many years later, the hole is still there, covered by a tarp of hope stretched tight. The hole that brought mind fire, the one that broke my head. I have neither time nor funds for nervous breakdowns. So I serve Jesus and write books. Even so, my rear refuses to stay covered. Thankfully, He's sent friends to cover me.

"I would like to go to that conference, but what will I say, what will I wear?" I said to her. My voice sounded empty, tired.

"You can't go with your butt hanging out. Maybe next year, you know? The book isn't out, the garment ain't made," my friend Gail replied, having no idea what she was really saying.

I hung my head. "I think God wants me to go. I just don't know . . ."

There was a pause on the line. "All right. I'll cover you. Watch the mail."

And so she covered me with clothes the way my friend Claudia covers me with words, with prayers. The way my friend Joy covers me with good food and fellowship, the way my friend Nancy celebrates my babies. The way my mother clothes my family, sending a box when it's most needed. So many sistahs the Lord has brought to comfort me and cover me when needed. And I'm thankful for all of them.

We always need someone to hold up our hands, but there's nothing like having sistahs who'll cover your backside. I keep learning from each of them because I want to be that kind of friend.

When my firstborn comes for me, with those wide, wise eyes, if she'll let me, I want to cover her too.

Father God, thank You for going back and covering the places in our lives where someone pointed and whispered instead of holding things closed. Help us to be coverers and comforters as we come into the full bloom of our lives. In Jesus's name, amen.

The Short Trip Back to Sanctuary

Davidae Stewart

Splendor and majesty are before him;
strength and glory are in his sanctuary.

PSALM 96:6 NIV

"Why can't you come home with me, baby doll?" Daddy asked me as we stood near the battered women's shelter van outside a community center in Georgia.

The shelter had designated the center as a safe place for us to meet. My roommates needed clothes, diapers, medical vouchers, and other necessities there.

And I needed my dad.

Daddy had searched for me all over town for two weeks; he almost killed my boyfriend when he thought the worst had happened to me.

But the worst *had* happened to me. I was homeless, pregnant, and afraid for my life. And if my boyfriend knew about the baby . . . my situation would become much worse. I'd run to the battered women's shelter to protect not only me and the baby, but my family, and most important, Daddy.

The last thing that oozed from my boyfriend's clenched teeth was, "I'll cut your daddy in half and slice your mother's throat, if you leave me."

And because of the slit he put on my right arm, I believed him.

You can't imagine how terrorized I felt walking around town hand in hand with a demon. That's what I believed happened to him, that something had possessed him, because he wasn't violent during the first seven years we knew each other. Something changed him. And I feared for his soul. I feared for my life.

Over time, my health began to fade. I couldn't concentrate at work. I couldn't eat or sleep. I needed medical attention, but the man was so possessed at the time that he wouldn't let me make a phone call without his permission. I couldn't go anywhere, not even take a lunch break without him.

My boss noticed the changes in me and came to me one morning.

"Dee, I want to pray for you," he said.

I pretended to pray with him, knowing full well that I would never tell him what was going on in my life. I knew people who'd lost their jobs over madness like this. So I kept my head bowed, kept my shame inside, and prayed to make it through the day without looking suspicious anymore.

It didn't work. My appetite disappeared. My body began to reject the spiritual poison that I had put inside. Something had to stop.

I prayed for a sign.

My dad called at work and said he wanted me to come to the house and pick up some barbecued chicken he had grilled the day before. (I hadn't been allowed to go to the family cookout.) This chance was my sign.

As I drove to Dad's a voice in my head—the Holy Spirit—told me, "Don't go to your dad's. Don't go home."

Without hesitation, I drove to the police department, walked inside, and asked to be placed in a battered women's shelter . . . a sanctuary.

Once there, I found out I was four months pregnant and was too afraid to leave the shelter.

So here Dad and I stood—after all of that—our feet sinking into the sweet-potato colored Georgia clay, afraid to look at one another, afraid to talk about what happened to me. Stuck. He was ashamed of not being able to protect me; I was ashamed of getting myself in this predicament in the first place.

"When are you coming home?" he asked again.

My heart skipped. I kicked the clay dirt underneath my feet, trying to keep from crying. "It's not safe for us. Not until the police find him. He-he-he said he'd kill you and so . . ."

The others were getting back in the van now, and I didn't want them to hear our conversation. I didn't want to break down.

Daddy mumbled something, threw his cigarette on the ground, and walked back toward his truck. "You tell those people that I'm coming to get you this afternoon."

"But, Daddy, I need a restraining order before I can leave," I almost yelled.

"I'll kill him if you don't come home," he yelled back, but didn't turn around.

I knew he was crying.

So as I took the short trip back to my sanctuary, I did something I hadn't done in three years, not since I met a man and forgot whom I belonged to. I repented.

I had to. I had to repent to God for not listening to Daddy, my uncles, and my mother, who had taught me that I was worth more than this mess. That God made me better than this situation, this man, and this abuse. I had to repent to God for not putting Him first, for not loving Him enough, for not loving myself enough, for not believing in His love that held me all my life. I had to repent and let it all go. I had to find sanctuary inside my soul. I had to prepare to take care of my unborn child without a father.

And then I heard a whisper. It was my social worker. "Your father just called the center. And they called me on my cell. Your dad is with his lawyer at the courthouse, getting you a restraining order, honey. Once you get back to the shelter, gather your belongings. I'll take you there to meet him."

My body trembled. Not because of fear, but because then I knew God had forgiven me. He made my father my guardian angel and I didn't realize it until then.

All these years later, my father's example still serves as a living witness that God's paternity isn't about fear and control, but about safety, provision, and unconditional love. No condemnation. No shame. Just love.

Father God, we thank You for placing earthly fathers on the earth who love their daughters. Even though we all haven't had that kind of daddy, we thank You for being our Daddy. Keep us safe, Lord, under your everlasting arms. In Jesus's name, amen.

Tamar's Wings

Marilynn Griffith

I was ultraviolet, radiating the brilliance of winter's first snow—
inviolate and unprofaned.
Then leviathan swept me from the heavens,
spilling my sunshine onto unwashed linoleum.

Aspiring to save at least the moon-juice,
warmed by a thousand suns and poured into the prism between
my diamond eyes,
I struggled to shine. Alas, it was too late.
I was opaque now and fading fast.

Plummeting, I tried to snatch a
rainbow from the bottom of his shoe,
but he laughed, swallowed it whole.
I saw a star stuck between his teeth.
I leapt for it to the crescendo of shadows
as he drank the dregs of my bright-eyed childhood.

He slinked away, leaving the dirge of shame churning in my ears.
I tried to smother it with my virtue, shredded and impotent,
but the charcoal sieved through it, staining every cell.

I crawled back to my room screaming.
Go back to sleep, they said.
I dried my eyes and tried to scrape the night,
funky and thick, from between my toes.

Eventually, I forgot my blaze and danced after midnight
for firecrackers and holy water.
Sometimes I saw a burning man beside me,
whispering my old name.

One night He caught me exposed. Dying.
He offered a hunk of flesh and a shot of blood.
Incredulous and desperate, I took and ate.

To my surprise, beams of light, fat and ridiculous,
shot from my face igniting into a sunrise.
A mask of sooty madness crashed in
seven-eighths time at my feet.

I fly now in daytime, spectrum magnificent,
looking for little girls in three-piece suits
with black stains they try to scrub
when no one is looking.

Twelve Weeks of Truth —Week Nine

Above all, love each other deeply,
because love covers over a multitude of sins.

1 PETER 4:8 NIV

DISCUSSION QUESTIONS

1. While shame often needs to be unmasked, there are times when a woman just needs covering. I walked around with my gown hanging open in the spirit for many years because those two women at the hospital should have covered me. I didn't realize it until a friend heard the story and got choked up. Now, if I'm not careful, it's easy for me to do the same thing: point a finger from a safe distance. While you can't save everyone, there will be women whom God brings into your life so that you can help in some way. Purpose in your heart to help those women in whatever way you can. Write out a prayer for those sistahs in need of covering.

2. We've all had enough of church cover-ups and fake faces, but there are times when something is just too raw, too painful to be exposed. Have you ever had to cover something so that it could heal? Have you ever gone through this with a friend?

3. Who has God used to be a rearguard in your life? Whose rearguard are you? If you think you know, tell her that you've got her back. She'll likely be glad to hear it.

Father God, we thank You for being our defense. Thank You for the women You put in our lives to cover our wounds until they can heal. Help me to do the same for other sistahs. In Jesus's name, amen.

CHAPTER TEN

CHOOSE LIFE

"I call heaven and earth to witness against you today, that I have set before you life and death, the blessing and the curse. So choose life in order that you may live, you and your descendants . . ."

DEUTERONOMY 30:19 NASB

Tamar had no way to hide her virgin garments, torn and soiled. She was defiled in the eyes of her brethren, through no fault of her own. Today's woman has a way to hide her secrets, to make no choice at all while others choose themselves. There is no evidence of the act, nothing that shows the life that was once held inside, but for all her days, a woman knows that she has done something terrible, something that though forgiven is rarely forgotten. There are no voting records here, no picket lines, just women who at least once in their lives felt helpless and hopeless enough to offer their children to the grave. Though abortion can be a hot topic for debate, this chapter isn't about politics, it's about people. People who, except for the grace of God, could have been you. People, who despite all your efforts to hide, might be you. Either way, listen to the voices of our sistahs as they clang on the story pot, beneath the beat of their song is another strain, the hum of God's shameless and enduring grace.

Tea and Crackers

Dr. Gail M. Hayes

You prepare a table before me in the presence of my enemies.

PSALM 23:5 NIV

These days, I see God's love in the smallest things. One morning, while watching a praise tape, I marveled as my two-year-old daughter worshipped the Lord. She blew on her toy clarinet, moving with the music, caught up in the wind of His power. It was simply beautiful. The Lord immersed me in the flood of His love with my baby. Looking at this scene, it was hard to believe that it was not so long ago that the thought of even having a child made me cringe.

As the firstborn girl of seven children, the last thing I wanted was a child. My main job was to help my mother with my six siblings. I changed and washed diapers, potty trained, cooked, cleaned, helped with homework, and combed hair. I felt emotionally tired most of the time. When I expressed my feelings, comments about tiredness being a normal state for women hit me hard. I was told and taught to "suck it up" and move on. This put a stranglehold on my heart, and I became a walking sack of emotional deadness.

As a young adult, all I wanted was complete freedom from these responsibilities. I wanted nothing to do with the family thing. I wanted time to find out who I was and what I wanted. I wanted freedom to do what I wanted, when I wanted, and how I wanted. I wanted to find me and a place where I felt valued. I found my value in the wrong place.

Then without warning, my newfound freedom collided with the brick wall of my actions' consequences. At age twenty-two, I discovered that I was pregnant. The last thing I wanted was a baby, especially since I was also unmarried at the time. Just the thought of night cries, bottle runs, and tiny helplessness made me nauseated. I decided to terminate the pregnancy. I wanted the parasite out of my body.

Yes, I called the life growing within me a parasite. I did not know the Lord. He was just that white man on the picture with the lambs under his arms to me. My experience with white people had not always been pleasant, so I wondered why people, especially black people, got so excited about Jesus.

I also hated myself and everyone else, so how could I feel anything for this child? I entered the abortion clinic wanting a quick and easy solution. The counselor was all too happy to explain that this was not a human life but merely a glob of tissue that they could easily clean out of my body.

This would be a simple procedure, she said. She took my money and covered my fear with smiles and undressed me with deceit. I submitted myself and this "glob" to the abortionist's hand. Afterward, they served me tea and crackers. I ate, not realizing the high price I would later pay for that snack.

I felt great relief as I exited the clinic, vowing never to go through its doors again. In a few months, I moved away from the Washington, DC, area, hoping to start a new life, not realizing the devastating blow I'd dealt to my body and spirit.

Shortly after arriving in North Carolina, I discovered I was pregnant again. This time, things were different. I moved back home with my parents to attend school. The pressure of moving back home after being on my own for four years was such that I could not expose my condition without risking my sanity. This backward move stripped me of any dignity I had and, again, I became a child.

I stood in two worlds. Although I was an adult in age, because I returned to a place where I was not in control, I was again a child. Pain and humiliation were main menu items during those times. I could barely survive emotionally, so how could I even think of bringing a baby into that environment?

Again, I went to the abortionist. This time, something went wrong. The machine that performed the deed stopped in the midst of the procedure and made a noise that reminded me of a horror movie. Something—or someone—jammed the machine. There was a gurgling, wet smacking sound that reminded me of a water vacuum that suddenly tried to swallow a mouse.

I felt an intense cramping and tried to sit up but couldn't. When the doctor asked the nurse to assist him, I again tried to sit up to see what was happening. The nurse slammed me back down on the table, but not before I saw the doctor's bloodied wrists. I felt sick and wanted to die. As they escorted me to my cushiony recliner, I put my hands between my legs to catch my violated uterus in case it decided to fall out onto the floor.

Just like the baby I had just killed, the experience left me mutilated. The results of this visit were a suicide attempt and a deep self-loathing I would be unable to shake for many years. This was payment for the second helping of tea and crackers.

After my "clinical" experience, I caught the bus to class. I attended all my afternoon classes with blurred vision. Like a boat set adrift on a gloomy night, the foghorn of my accounting professor's voice cut through my senses with an irritating slowness, reminding me that I was still alive but half-dead.

After class, I stood at the bus stop for over an hour as my knees violently shook from the weight of my saturated emotions. During the ninety-minute ride home, I slept, only to be awakened by the gushing between my aching legs, the only remaining sign of what really happened to me that day.

That night, I slept hard. Hard enough to push back the memory of the day. Hard enough to swallow the sights and sounds of what I had just done. Hard enough to become a new hard me. The next morning, I felt victorious since I had successfully suffocated my pain, anger, fear, and any motherly feelings I had with my pillow. I was now free and clear to navigate life again. Free and clear to embrace the numbness that now occupied and ruled my emotional plane. Free and clear to encase myself in a cocoon of sexual perversion, anger, and silent screams. I would find no relief from this place until I discovered the miraculous.

The miraculous I found was Jesus. I discovered that He was not the man in that picture. He was not just someone who held lambs . . . He held me! When I also discovered I was grieving for those lost children, Jesus made me a promise. He told me that He would restore them to me.

I was also only having one or two menstrual cycles each year. I learned that I had a physically closed womb. My doctor told me she believed that my body had protected itself from my previous trauma and a membrane now covered my cervix. She wanted to surgically remove the membrane. Since my doctor wanted the surgery, I had to tell my husband, who was not the father of those babies, about the abortions. After hearing the details, he said no man would cut me. If God closed my womb, then He would open it. I rejoiced, although I knew in my heart he wanted to be a father. I still danced daily with fear.

Many years later, the day after my fortieth birthday, I decided that I was tired of the dance. I had a complete change of heart. The Lord did another miraculous thing for this girl. My husband really wanted children, so I put aside my selfish desires, fell on my face, and asked the Lord to open my physically closed womb.

After eleven years of being barren, within two months of that prayer, I discovered I was pregnant. At age forty-one, my precious Father allowed me to give birth to a strong, handsome son. At age forty-three He again rained down His grace and gave my husband and me a daughter of the King.

He restored my lost children to me. Tears of unspeakable joy fill my eyes when tiny arms encircle my neck. With each hug, fragments of yesterday's torment vanish. With each kiss, healing balm fills my once broken heart.

This is the depth of His love. He restored everything taken by the darkness of my past. He shined His light on the hidden treasures buried in my soul and gave me a future and a hope. He enveloped me in the sea of His love and washed me in the wave of His awesome forgiveness. My cup overflows with promises for my future. He anointed me with oil, draped me in royal robes, and placed a crown upon my head. I am His daughter, a daughter of the King.

His word says He removes our sin far from us. Because of His mercy, I stand unashamed of my past. Because of His loving kindness, I pray for those caught in abortion's deadly trap. I pray that, like me, they will one day stand in the mighty flow of God's love and not consume another snack of tea and crackers. Today, I stand waiting to wipe fear's crumbs from hurting mouths and dry lips, dripping with guilt's tea. I stand waiting to love someone into the kingdom.

Father God, I thank You for Your mercy and Your restoring power. Restore to us all the things we've destroyed, all the things that were stolen. We declare You miraculous and thank You for anointing our heads with the oil of gladness every day. May we wear it like queens! In Jesus's name, amen.

No Choice

Marilynn Griffith

The marchers walk over faded sidewalks in an elliptical path,
signs held high, frowns firm, demanding that she
turn around/choose life/just say No.

I stare at her, reading her hurt, in cold and wounded eyes.
Eyes that tell me that she did say No,
but learned quickly the word's feebleness,
echoing her own weakness back in her ears, burning in her
throat, unheeded.
Now, her eyes said, she says nothing,
only turns to the wall,
counting moldy roses on basement wallpaper.

My sign, already half-mast, knocks against my shoulder
as she darts inside.
The oblong trail pauses, the chants die to a whisper.
The volume resumes.

Another girl is coming.
I step back, praying now.
For her. For us. For me.
For the writers of empty rhetoric like pro-life and pro-choice.

She sees no life and no choice,
since the robber/liar/thief begged/robbed/stole her only treasure.
Neither did I.

I cry for her, knowing that one day,
she will grow up and find a stray diamond left between her
thighs,
and realize
she had a choice after all.

Chapter Ten: Choose Life

Amazed by Grace

Stanice Anderson

*The Lord upholds all those who fall,
And raises up all who are bowed down.
The eyes of all look expectantly to You,
And You give them their food in due season.
You open Your hand
And satisfy the desire of every living thing.*

PSALM 145:14–16 NKJV

The long shiny black thin bent wire, which only minutes before hung in the closet with her starched white nurse's uniform, was now a makeshift surgical instrument. Her long dark fingers threaded the cylindrical tubing onto the wire as she held it up to the kitchen ceiling light.

"What's that?" I asked.

"Don't worry," she replied. "Relax and drink the nice hot tea I made for you." I lay there on the hard kitchen table cushioned only by a ragged white sheet.

I reached for the cup, drank the tea, and allowed my question to drown in the bittersweet taste.

Fellow students told me she was a nurse and could take care of our "little problem" for the three hundred dollars that we managed to put together out of our college allowances. These same people said, "It'll be over before you know it. No pain. You'll be back in class on Monday."

I concentrated on those comforting words from well-meaning friends. I blotted out everything else, including the life that was about to die inside of me. I was fourteen weeks pregnant and a freshman whose dad had just paid second-semester tuition.

I felt groggy. The room started to spin. The bright overhead lightbulb had spikes of reds and blues that darted about the ceiling like fireflies. It had to be the tea. I tried to rise from the table. My head felt like a block of lead. "What was in that tea?"

"Just lay back and shut up." Her words grabbed me by the throat and held me captive. "You college whores have your fun and then you come to me to help you get rid of your little problems."

This couldn't be the same nurse. Someone else must have come into the room; but I saw only one figure bent over me. I struggled to get up. I couldn't. With one hand she pushed down on my chest and with the other she probed my most private of parts. These were hands that were supposed to comfort the sick—now they were lethal weapons. She picked up the wire.

I felt excruciating stabbing pains deep inside me. I screamed, "Stop!" but something cold and clammy was over my mouth. The room faded to black.

How long I lay there I don't know. What happened after the wire? I don't know. The pain, I remember; it felt like someone had taken a red-hot poker and ripped my insides. The sheet was cold and wet with blood. The silence in the house, I remember. A note on the chair beside the table read, "Take these antibiotics; one every eight hours. Call your boyfriend. Be gone before I get back."

I felt so weak. My body screamed for painkillers. "God give me strength," I prayed. I tried to walk, but I couldn't stand up straight. I dropped to the floor and found that crawling was less painful. I pulled the phone to the floor and called my boyfriend. "Come and get me," I said.

He took me back to the dorm; then he and a girlfriend tried to keep me quiet, but I was in so much pain. The pillow wasn't drowning my moans. They decided to take me to a motel. We checked into a room on the back side of the motel and they helped me in.

The room was suspiciously dim, yet the water-stained wallpaper was still visible. The ramshackle wood dresser sagged in the middle. Over the bed hung a picture painted on black velvet of a matador teasing a charging bull.

My girlfriend draped the bed with plastic dry cleaner bags and trash bags and lay me down. I rocked, reeled, cried, and hollered into a musty pillow for hours. Something was definitely wrong. My girlfriend, who had also experienced an abortion, guided us through the process.

"When will the pain stop?" I asked. I must have asked her that a hundred times.

"Soon. Soon," she said.

"Take me to the hospital. I don't want to die," I pleaded.

"No, we can't do that," my boyfriend said. Abortion was illegal. Every few hours they would take me into the bathroom and have me sit straddled on the toilet seat facing the dingy, cracked wall.

"Push," my friend said.

I pushed. I felt pain in every part of my body. It hurt to talk, move, or breathe. I was also losing a lot of blood.

Exactly twenty-three hours after we left the nurse's house, they took me to the toilet seat again. I straddled and pushed. A pain hit me unlike all the others. I felt like my body was exploding from the inside out; then, I heard *plop!* in the water below me. Almost immediately, I saw the dead tiny brown curved baby floating in the little pond of blood and water. My knees buckled. My heart ripped. My mind took a photograph that would be developed again and again for many years.

I learned at that moment what regret meant. It was no longer an abstract word but had substance and form, and a heart that would never beat again because of me.

If only my story ended there . . . but it didn't: It was only the beginning. If you've determined that a legal abortion would have eliminated my pain and suffering, think again.

Before that twenty-third hour, I knew no real pain. The real pain begins when the life is ended. Real pain lingers, night after sleepless night. When sleep comes, I revisit that straddle-stool in my dreams. Most days, I would rather be hit in the head with a hammer than think about what happened that night; I would at least know that the pain would stop.

Often, I wonder, "What would my child look like?" "Was it a girl or a boy?" "How old would my child be now?" Just seeing the father or my girlfriend reminded me of our secret. Passing the town or hearing the state's name brought back memories I wanted desperately to forget.

Those well-meaning friends didn't tell me how to live with the decision to abort. Neither parties, drugs, lovers, geographical changes, nor the passing years ever dulled the pain.

Then one day, I listened to a radio broadcast, a dramatic reading of a novella entitled *Tilly*, by Frank E. Peretti. The story is about a woman whose aborted child returns to comfort her. The little girl assures her that she's all right and with God in heaven. She also tells her mom that when her mom asked for forgiveness a long time ago, God heard her and forgave her. Now she just had to forgive herself, and know that one day they would be together again. I listened and wept. My heart pounded and suddenly I recalled a verse that I didn't remember ever memorizing: "If we confess our sins, he is faithful and just and will forgive us and cleanse us from all unrighteousness." Later, I found out that it was 1 John 1:9.

At that moment, I felt that I had carried the emotional pain of my decision to abort long enough. My feelings about the abortion were bitter roots that had to be pulled up and thrown out. They were getting in the way of living my life to the fullest on this new road that I was determined to stay on. I knew that if I didn't let go, I would eventually use drugs again to numb the pain. I knew that I would continue to have nightmares and feel sadness whenever I looked at children. I knew that I could not be joyful in my present or future if I continued to cling to the things of the past. The deed was done. I did it and I could not undo it. But the story that I heard on the radio that day, combined with the verse that came into my mind, gave me hope and convinced me that God would forgive me, if I asked.

So I got on my knees and cried out to God, "Please, forgive me."

In the next moment, I felt the burden I had carried in my mind and heart for over twenty years lifted. I knew He heard my prayer because the never-ending pain was replaced with a perfect peace that I had never known, deep down on the inside where my spirit resides. I lingered there on my knees, afraid that if I stood up the peace would dissipate. But God sealed His peace with assurance as I prayerfully talked to my baby, saying, "Please forgive me for not allowing you to live a full life."

In the stillness of my mind, I replayed the story of Tilly but imagined my own child saying, "I forgive you, Mama. I'll see you one day and never have to say good-bye."

Still on my knees and with tears flowing from the slits of my closed eyes, I whispered, "How will I know you?"

"You don't have to know what I look like. You're my mother. I'll know you."

I knelt there and absorbed the love I felt like a thirsty sponge. It was as if she hugged me and then cradled my tear-stained face in her small, soft hands and kissed my tears away.

I slowly stood up, not wanting to leave the moment. But it's a moment in my life that will forever far outweigh the pain that I carried for so many years. A new peace was sealed with an image in my mind of a touch of assurance and a healing kiss from my aborted child.

I've not forgotten that night. Now and again, I think of my child in heaven. Years later, when my son proudly strode across the stage to get his college degree, I whispered into my hand, "Aren't you proud of your brother?"

"Yes, Mama, I am."

I understand that some men and women feel no residual emotional trauma from choosing to abort, but for those of us who are still haunted by our past decisions, we can let go now. We can't undo what we did but we can go to God with anything and everything, because He cares. We can ask for forgiveness, receive it, and then forgive ourselves so that we can move on with the plan that God has for our lives.

Also, I've found that because I had this experience, God brought many women and men along my path with whom I can share the answers and comfort that I found. As we are healed, we will be able to understand and empathize with others because we have been there. Thus, it gives our lives even more meaning and purpose. Our struggles will not have been in vain.

God has turned my hurts into compassion for others as well as given me joy in knowing that His forgiveness is real and lasts a lifetime. The same thing that God has done for me He is willing to do for you.

Dear Heavenly Father: We come to You believing that You can and will heal the inner wounds that the world can't see. We lift our gaping emotional and spiritual wounds up to You. Heal us.

Make us whole and free. We are tired of carrying burdens that keep us from moving into the plan that You have in mind for our lives. Regrets only pull us down to the ground, where we lie, moan, and groan because of the sheer magnitude of our past choices. We lay our hurts and our falling short of what You would have us to do at your feet. Forgive us and continue to take care of our children until one day You bring us home to You and we will see them again and never have to say goodbye. Thank You that You hear our prayers and that it is done as we have asked. Use us to comfort others as You have so graciously comforted us. Amen. So be it!

Reprinted by permission from Stanice Anderson, *I Say a Prayer for Me: One Woman's Life of Faith and Triumph* (Walk Worthy Press/ Warner Books), © 2002.

Evergreen

Marilynn Griffith

Turn me to my yellow leaves,
I am better satisfied;
There is something in me grieves—
That was never born, and died.
Let me be a scarlet flame
On a windy autumn morn,
I who never had a name,
Nor from breathing image born.
From the margin let me fall
Where the farthest stars sink down,
And the void consumes me,—all
In nothingness to drown.
Let me dream my dream entire,
Withered as an autumn leaf—
Let me have my vain desire,
Vain—as it is brief.

"Turn Me to My Yellow Leaves" by William Stanley Braithwaite, *The Book of American Negro Poetry*, 1922

How I long to be evergreen, staunch and determined, instead of curling in on myself, a yellowed, crunchy leaf. I do that sometimes, especially in autumn. Though I haven't witnessed the birth of an Ohio fall in many years, though I live far away in a warm place, the cool blows through me still. In these times, all my seeds, my never born, or born and gone, come back to me, drawing my knees up in the wake of winter.

The fall of 2004 was no different. In fact, it might have been a little worse. In spite of my favorite lipstick and the sweet drape of my best scarf, I felt the chill, the crunch and bite of soul-cold, threatening my bone-fire. If not for Christ's hands cupped round my small flame, not for His lush grace like a carpet between my feet, my flicker might have been extinguished, barren of word and prayer.

Thank God that He is evergreen.

I am no such thing and once was so much worse. That year, that fall, it felt much, much worse. The Day of Atonement rang true to me then, gave me pause during the Rosh Hashanah hush. Though I was not born Jewish—just grafted in by Christ—the ancient celebrations are a comfort. Especially when yesterdays rush up around my eyes, filling my head with memories of waiting rooms with wide-eyed women twisting their wedding rings and girls in tennis bracelets holding hands with their embarrassed fathers. And me, alone. Always alone.

They'd drop me off, pick me up, but never stay. Not my friends, not my boyfriends, not my mother. Though it wasn't really "wrong," they said, nobody wanted to bloody their hands or watch me cry, see me make for the door and come stumbling back out, begging God for another chance even though there seemed to be none. Nobody watched me glisten auburn, burn copper, blaze gold . . . and then curl up on the edges of my soul. Dry.

That fall, in 2004, my Jewell, the baby I gave away, the one who started it all, became a grown woman. I prayed for her then, hoping she'd be wise and good, godly and strong. I pray for her now, hoping that if I meet her this side of heaven she won't be ashamed. And the others? I see them in my dreams, long-limbed and luscious with black-eyed Susan eyes. They smile and wave, knowing that I can take that now, that in spite of my thin-veined heart and yellowed pain, I can wave back. Smile at them. I can't do it really, but He can. For He is always strong.

> He is evergreen.
> He will be like a tree planted by the water
> that sends out its roots by the stream.
> It does not fear when heat comes;
> its leaves are always green.

It has no worries in a year of drought
and never fails to bear fruit.
—Jeremiah 17:8 NIV

Father God, thank You for being faithful, even when I falter. Thank You for being always lush and green and ready to grow new things in me. May Your healing power break forth in every season of my life. In Jesus's name, amen.

Twelve Weeks of Truth
—Week Ten

Here am I, and the children the LORD has given me.
We are signs and symbols in Israel from the LORD Almighty,
who dwells on Mount Zion.

ISAIAH 8:18 NIV

DISCUSSION QUESTIONS

1. Did any of the stories in this chapter give you a better understanding of a woman who has had an abortion? If you have had an abortion yourself, were any of the stories true to your experience? If you feel ready, discuss this with the group, with the direct understanding that all things discussed in the SistahFaith Circle are confidential.

2. Many women today have experienced an abortion but have never truly dealt with the situation. How do you think secrets affect a woman, especially concerning abortion?

3. Though we may not have received them at the time they were first given to us all our children are given to us by God. What can we do each day to teach our children—boys and girls—the importance of life?

Pray this prayer together:

Father God, we thank You for life. Help us to choose life more often. Help us to allow our wounds to heal so that we can be free of secrets and all the pain that goes with it. In Jesus's name, amen.

CHAPTER ELEVEN

GARMENTS OF PRAISE

And provide for those who grieve in Zion—
to bestow on them a crown of beauty instead of ashes,
the oil of gladness
instead of mourning,
and a garment of praise
instead of a spirit of despair.

ISAIAH 61:3 NIV

Though shame can grip tight at our hearts the way it did Tamar's, God receives us from the hands of our sistahs, crowning us with beauty for the ashes of our expectations. For the tears, for the things that could have been, he anoints us with the oil of gladness, removing the black streaks worn by those who grieve. We have shared our stories and heard the stories of others. Though our virginal garments were soiled and torn, God, the best fashion designer, gives us a new outfit—the garment of praise.

Let despair and shame slide off your shoulders. Step out of your pain and into the hands of God. He saw. He heard. He knows. Your sistahs know too. Accept this new dress of kindness and grace, this praise that leaves you transparent yet covered. Take it, sistah, and wear it well.

If I Were Her

Claudia Mair Burney

You did not give me a kiss, but this woman, from the time I entered, has not stopped kissing my feet.

LUKE 7:45 NIV

I walk up to the house, and the oil I have, lavender, the best thing I could afford, is in my hand. Frankly, I'd probably have chosen lavender even if I could afford spikenard. He knows this about me, and, I think, it'll mean more to Him. He's like that. He always loves you in the way He loves *you.* He makes you feel special. For Him, you are special. I smile when I remember this about Him.

I'm honest with myself that I'm not comfortable. These are *good* people at this gathering. Successful, religious, upstanding, and I don't begrudge them that. I just don't like the way they look down on me. They talk. They tsk-tsk. They feel sorry for me, and I hate that the most.

I'm not here for them. I steel myself. I'm here for Him. I make myself remember that. I think about this conversation I had with Him, and it's all about me flirting with men. He looks at me. He's got those eyes that look right into you. Not exotic eyes. They are simple brown eyes, but when He looks at you He *sees* you, and oh, the love in those eyes! Even in that conversation about me flirting inappropriately. He looks at me and says, "What are you doing?" And I say, "Oh." It is a tiny, breathy *oh* that catches in my throat. It is not an interjection of understanding, it's an involuntary utterance, and I shake my head because something inside feels loose and fragile, and I want to cry, and I want to hug Him, but all I say is that little *oh* and smile a strange, half, not-really-a-smile smile, because He's caught me. He knows my game and calls me on it.

"I just want to be loved," I say, and I don't mean to be this truthful, but He always draws awful honesty out of me with His simple questions. As usual, He's gotten to the point straightaway, and in answer, He says, "You *are* loved." That's all He says, and it's enough.

I open the door and walk inside the house. I see a man I know only too well. I walk past him. I'm not here for him. Jesus is in the room.

I see Him. I'm across the room, and like radar, He detects me, and turns. The people grow quiet as they follow His eyes. What's got Jesus's attention? I can tell they can't believe it's me. Again, I think to myself, *I'm not here for them.*

I'm five feet away. Those eyes, they are so tender. I start choking up and stop. I don't want to cry. I just want to touch Him. I want to thank Him. He didn't abandon me. He didn't disappoint me. He loved me, and here's the thing, He taught me that I could love a man without an agenda. I'm nervous, because I don't touch Him when we meet, but I will on this night. I want Him to be the first man I've ever touched without some head game. And what's more, I don't want to abandon Him, or disappoint Him, either.

He lifts His face, just barely, but I notice it. He's beckoning me forward, and I come. I want to do this beautifully, but I don't. I am clumsy when I pour oil on His head, but He doesn't flinch. I wipe it through His hair, and I move closer, so I can smell the way his hair smells. It is sweaty. It smells like Him. I like the way He smells.

I plop down on the floor, the only grace between us being His. I don't care that it hurts my knees. I start bawling like a baby and I'm not sure why. I rub the oil between my hands, and I can't see because I'm crying so hard. This is not a beautiful gesture. It is raw and aching and terrible and amazing. He just sits there, oblivious to the stares and whispers, and there's an outcry or two. He just lets me rub his feet, and kiss them, and smell the sweet and musky scent of lavender. I don't sexualize this moment, because it is Him. It is my Jesus, and this moment is the prologue to my deliverance.

I love Him. I love Him. I love Him. And I cry so hard that snot falls from my nose and tears from my eyes onto His feet. I can't stop. I love Him. And I didn't think to bring tissues, because I wanted to be poised and elegant, but I'm a mess. I don't even think to wipe my tears with my clothes. I wash his feet, using my hair. My hair is very short and kinky curly. Afro hair, with just a touch of something straighter and finer, but not much. I don't know if it tickles Him. If it does, He doesn't let on.

He doesn't touch me back.

I believe it's because it was my time to do the touching. I think if I ever stop crying and get up, things will be different for me. I can touch without the stain of evil, impossible to cleanse. I can love with some measure of purity. Maybe I'm not perfect, but He's taught me something big here tonight. He taught me that I am not a whore. I am not a breeder. His love is His hands. I am touched by His love.

When I can rise, I stand and look at Him, and there are those eyes again. I am still crying, but now I am laughing through my tears, and I am so happy, and He laughs with me. He is my laughter. My Lord.

I bow to Him, kissing His feet one last time. It is a long, lingering kiss that I don't want to end. It is time for me to leave. I walk out of the house, and the night air is warm and moist. It's like walking in a cloud. Fireflies light the nighttime sky like a string of Christmas lights. I don't care what they say about me when I leave. He loves me. He loves me.

He will remember me.

Always.

Father God, thank You for letting us close to You and not caring when we kiss your feet with praise. May we always be mindful of how precious You are. Glory to the Lamb of God! In Jesus's name, amen.

Two Minutes

Dr. Gail M. Hayes

*And how shall they preach unless they are sent? As it is written:
"How beautiful are the feet of those who preach the gospel of peace,
Who bring glad tidings of good things!"*

ROMANS 10:15 NKJV

I was irritated. I took a deep breath and pulled the phone closer to my ear.

"Gail, Jesus loves you. I know you don't believe it but He does. I can hardly wait to see what He does with your life. You have a gift. You are what others call a persuader of people. God is going to use that gift one day for His glory."

For His glory? What kind of talk is that? She must really be crazy. God does not do the same things today that He did in the Bible. Those things were for the Bible days. A persuader of people? Pleeeze! I can't even persuade my family to accept me. How am I supposed to persuade anyone to do anything? Questions raced through my mind like a whirlwind.

Once again, my younger sister was telling me about Jesus and getting on my nerves. I cringed every time she spoke that way. There was a time, not so long ago, when she and I could talk about things, but she had changed since becoming a committed Christian.

How could she get so excited about this person called Jesus? To me, He was the white man with lambs under His arms. His haunting face was a permanent fixture on the family Bible that my mother kept on the coffee table in our living room.

As a person who had just broken the gender barrier by becoming the first African-American female law enforcement officer in her city, I did not understand my sister's excitement. I was fighting for survival in world dominated by white men who daily let me know that I was stealing the job of another man who had a family. I believed that her babbling about Jesus did little to impact me, so I allotted her two minutes. Little did I know how those two minutes would one day change my life.

Although I had grown up in a churchgoing family, I believed that I would go to heaven because I was nice to everyone. My mother took us to Sunday school. I heard the stories and even sang the songs. Still, nothing moved or convinced me. I believed that since I tried to treat everyone fairly, I was not one of those sinners mentioned in the hymns. I didn't have a clue that I was standing at hell's fiery gates and could have very easily been the gatekeeper.

At the time of my sister's phone conversations with me, I was an adulteress. I was involved with a married man. I wanted him to give her up but he refused. He was my addiction, so I continued in the relationship. I would pull him closer, hoping for a change, and then I would suddenly push him away and tell him that I never wanted to see him again. I struggled with emotional bouts of tears and self-torture, telling myself this is all I deserved.

"No man will ever want you. You will never get married." These words, spoken by my father during one of our many heated discussions, haunted me. They stood in the shadows and laughed at the brokenness of my femininity. I drifted through a sea of unhealthy relationships, never docking at stability's safe harbor. Rejection was my life's anchor, loneliness my perverted ally. So it hurt, but was not surprising, when my lover grew tired of the game, left, and got married. The day he returned from his honeymoon, we tearfully came together again and the affair intensified. It lasted for another four years.

In the midst of this sinful encounter, my sister accepted the Lord. I mean, she not only got saved, but she was crazy saved. She talked about the Lord all the time. You could experience God's power just from her conversations. She always wanted to talk about Jesus. Everything we talked about usually ended up with us discussing Him. I quickly grew tired of this and told her that she had two minutes to talk about Jesus. I was paying for the calls and only wanted to talk about my sinful relationships.

This tug-of-war went on for quite some time but she never gave up or became offended. She listened to the stories of my adultery and never judged me. Looking back, I remember her consistency. She used her two minutes wisely for God's purposes.

One night, a couple of hours after speaking with her, I went to bed feeling uneasy. After fighting a turbulent sleep for what seemed like hours, I got up and began cleaning my house. Everything felt dirty. I cleaned out closets and swept and mopped floors. I washed clothes and cleaned my bathrooms. I cleaned every room and washed every wall. I even took a shower because even my skin felt unclean.

After my shower, I began cleaning my bedroom and something strange happened. I took the sheets off the bed and, without knowing why, with bucket and sponge in hand, I furiously scrubbed and soaked the entire mattress. After the cleaning, I noticed that it was well into the early morning hours. I felt troubled and fearful, so I called my sister. She seemed alarmed and asked why I'd called at that hour. I wept as I told her about my cleaning. With tearful trembling, I told her how my heart ached with loneliness, how my life was a wreck, and that I could find no peace. I needed help but did not know where to look or where to begin.

In the midst of my weeping, I told her that I wanted what she had. I begged my sister to lead me to the Lord. I could no longer stand the void of hopelessness that surrounded me. I wanted joy and hope for my future. I dropped to my knees and leaned on the water-soaked mattress as my sister led me in prayer. I knelt in soapy water that washed clean the filth from my mattress. I arose, cleaned with the water of His word.

I left my lover and started living for the Lord. It was not easy being a Christian single. It was one of the hardest seasons of my life. I immediately started reading my Bible and praying with passion. I asked my Father to send a Christian husband . . . quickly! Within a year of leaving the adulterous relationship, a Christian man found and married me. That was over twenty years ago.

I thank God that my sister did not give up on me. Even when I seemed resistant to the message of the Gospels, she invested heavily in her two minutes. She prayed and spoke to me in boldness. She did not become offended by my barbs of opposition. She planted the seeds of God's mercy in my hungry soul, and when they germinated, they pushed through the soil of my resistance. The fragrance of His knowledge drew me to Him. The strength of His power, like a mighty flood, carried away my life's filthy debris and I became new.

I became a daughter of the King.

My sister's tenacity let me know to never stop praying and believing. It let me know that God will send the right person with the right message at the right time. Her prayers started a chain reaction of faith and salvation in my family. This prayerful chain is so powerful that it gave me a wonderful gift. After many years of experiencing turbulence in our relationship, it enabled me to lead my father to the Lord before he died. It enabled me to see my earthly father's love for me. It enabled me to forgive him. It enabled me to grasp the power of God's timing. For me, all He needed was two minutes.

Father God, we ask for the steadfastness to keep praying for those in our households, even when it seems they will not hear. Send the right people at the right time to water and reap a harvest among our loved ones. May we always remember that every soul is but seconds away from grace, including ourselves. In Jesus's name, amen.

My Heart Waketh

Marilynn Griffith

I sleep, but my heart waketh: it is the voice of my beloved that knocketh, saying, Open to me, my sister, my love, my dove, my undefiled: for my head is filled with dew, and my locks with the drops of the night.

SONG OF SOLOMON 5:2 KJV

I woke up this morning, remembering healed breaches and rebuilt walls. Thinking how in all my mess God had given me a brick, strong and brown, baked in the Caribbean sun. A solid thing of a man. It was he who looked past my dust and saw my wings, who had my back when I didn't even know I needed it.

Many people, even those who will never fly, had seen my wings before. But he wanted more than just to gawk. "Let me see. Turn around. Tell me everything."

That was an unexpected and unacceptable response. I ran. I screamed. Yet, I could not get off the ground. No matter how much of a head start I got, my feet stuck to the earth. Beside him.

"Why are you doing that? Running away?" he asked, picking Sharon roses and valley lilies and stuffing them in my pockets.

The flowers made me run faster, take another pass. "I have to leave, to fly away. But I can't. So you must go. Now, before it's too late."

He laughed at me. A chocolate, delicious laugh. I felt sick. How would I ever live without that sound?

"I'm not leaving," he said, winking one of those beautiful eyes. "So you might as well sit down." He did, as if for an example. "I love you."

My throat closed up. I hadn't escaped in time. Maybe he could still get away. I pushed him with my words, shoved him as hard as I could.

He didn't budge. "Stop it," he said as the insults hurled past him. "I love you."

"Don't love me. Please. You don't know what you're getting into. I'm crazy. I—" My wings released then, filled the room. He saw it all—pink, purple, gold, blue—the whole beautiful mess of me. I closed my eyes, knowing that when I opened them, he, like all the others, would be gone.

Blink. Peek.

He was still there, eating a pork chop. "Girl, please. Sit down. Let's talk. Communicate. That's what people do, you know. What kind of people have you been dealing with?"

You don't want to know.

Charles Barkley was on the TV. Boxing out, posting up, refusing to move. The Brown Mound of Rebound. Just like my man. He licked his fingers, smiled at me. I shuddered. What kind of game was this? Love? Please. He had to get out of here. Right now. And I knew just the thing.

I sat next to him. He took my hand, diluted my focus. "You ready to talk to me? To tell me what's wrong? It doesn't matter what it is. I can take it." He took another bite of pork chop, real close to the bone.

It would matter. It always did. I gave him a bittersweet smile, knowing this kindness would end. This wonder. "I'm pregnant."

He kept chewing, his twenty-year-old eyes still locked on the TV. "That's it? Just a baby? I thought you were dying or something." He took my hand and kissed it.

I stared at the barbecue sauce smeared on my skin. The hope in me, the fool that I thought long dead, yawned and stretched her legs. His heartbeat knocked at the door of me like police raiding a crack house. He put down his pork chop sandwich, stared at me, into me, with those talking eyes.

Open to me, my sister, my love, my dove, my undefiled.

My stomach turned as Hope rubbed her eyes, waking her long-slumbering sisters. Faith roused first, her kinky braids pointing in every direction.

Open the door, honey, she whispered. *You Know Who is out there too.*

He kissed my eyes. "It'll be okay. We can make it. God will help us."

Love sprang to her feet then, knocking me out of the way. Ran to the door of my heart at full speed. I thought I saw smoke swirling in through the cracks. I tried to call her back, to tell her she'd be burned, but she ran faster, grabbed the red-hot handle, and swung it wide.

The man I'd mistaken for a boy came in. His clothes were not burned. He didn't even smell like smoke. There was another with him, One with hair like white wool. One like the Son of Man.

I hung my head, but He held it up.

Fear not, the voice said.

But the baby isn't his, I replied wordlessly.

The answer shook my soul.

I know. The baby is mine.

With that, He was gone from sight, leaving me in a snug, brown embrace, showered with pork-chop-and-macaroni-and-cheese kisses. I knuckled the grit out of my eyes, out of my heart. Though it terrified me, it was good to be awake.

And now, seventeen years of marriage and seven children later, it is even better.

Father God, we thank You that perfect love casts out fear. Though we have been wounded, heal us in a way that when love comes, good and godly love, we will be able to accept it, especially from You. In Jesus's name, amen.

From Shame to Praise

Dee East

"Do not fear, for you will not be ashamed; Neither be disgraced, for you will not be put to shame; For you will forget the shame of your youth, And will not remember the reproach of your widowhood anymore. For your Maker is your husband . . ."

ISAIAH 54:4–5 NKJV

"Ah, Lord, what will this year bring? Will You bring something good into our lives? We need a change."

New Year's Eve 1975 was coming to a close. After a quiet dinner, I returned to my home to relieve the babysitter while my sons slept. As midnight approached, I poured a glass of wine for a toast, but I was more focused on prayer and a cry from my heart for change.

Almost six years into my journey of widowhood, my boys and I experienced a succession of dark days and nights. As much as I missed my husband, they missed their daddy. I tried to fill my evenings with activities meant to bring cheer into our lives. Yet we had little joy during those early years.

Shortly after my thirty-year-old husband's unexpected death, I bought a new home. I thought a fresh start would help, but this place lacked the warmth of our old home. My sons were the only children in our hundred-family neighborhood with no daddy. This became the source of taunts and unfounded speculation from thoughtless children.

"Your daddy's in prison," or "Your dad left you!" Scorn and contempt took their toll on three lonely boys. I knew that things had to change that New Year's Eve, but I didn't know how.

My widowhood occurred after less than ten years of marriage, and I knew of no widows close to my age with young children. I felt terribly alone. I had no respite from the responsibilities and care of my sons. My sorrows were profound, deep, and increased by concerns for my children. I tried to shield them so my boys would not feel so bereft and things would seem normal. My heart felt splintered, filled with unfulfilled memories of lost times, hopelessness, and anxiety for raising fatherless sons.

The answer came with a phone call the following Sunday afternoon. A new friend called me about her prayer group, one that had comforted her during a difficult situation. This intrigued me, so we met the following week. I discovered there that I could have a personal relationship with Jesus Christ, that I was never alone. I could bare my heart to Him, and He truly cared for me. His Word became my treasure.

As with any marriage, I have come to know our Lord more intimately through the years. My boys grew into men of God and now have children of their own. No longer needing a home for raising children, I traded yard work and home maintenance for a condominium with a view of a two-hundred-year-old oak tree I remembered from my childhood.

That tree had stood in the middle of a farm but was now surrounded by two condominium buildings. One unit I visited had a large room with cathedral ceilings perfect for my living and dining room furniture. I easily imagined this elegant room filled with smiling ladies in Bible study or sharing times. Isaiah 61:1–2 (NKJV) filled my mind's ear: "He has sent Me to heal the brokenhearted/To proclaim liberty to the captives . . . To comfort all who mourn." God often comforted me with those verses, and I felt it might be the place for me to encourage and help others.

It was the scene from the second-floor balcony that sold me—a breathtaking view of the two-hundred-year-old oak tree. As I greeted this old friend, Isaiah 61:3 affirmed, "To console those who mourn in Zion/To give them beauty for ashes/The oil of joy for mourning/The garment of praise for the spirit of heaviness/That they may be called trees [or oaks] of righteousness/The planting of the LORD, that He may be glorified."

The old oak now had picnic benches around its base, creating a delightful park area. Lights placed under its branches showcased its rare beauty night or day.

Thus began a marvelous season in that home. My life was filled with friends, Bible reading, and sharing times that fulfilled the vision I had as I first entered the room. Yes, there were occasions I also felt lonely and discouraged. At times I sensed the loneliness and loss of my husband in deep ways as if it had been yesterday rather than nearly thirty years before. My walk with Christ was precious, but sometimes loneliness and grief tried to rush in and inundate me.

One midwinter day, I felt extreme hopelessness, especially when I looked out at the tree. The branches were totally bare. Usually a few leaves remained on the branches until the spring sap pushed off the old ones, but this year strong winds and rain tore at them, and the tree seemed more barren than usual. While looking at the tree I started to think of the size of the roots under its span. I recalled reading that an oak tree's roots were often twice as long as the upward and outward growth. I envisioned the roots of that lovely oak tree growing deep into the soil, seeking water during dry seasons, even as the branches continually reached upward and outward.

I also recalled a move from a home for which we had a buyer wanting immediate occupancy. A large firethorn bush with lovely orange berries graced the yard. The branches had unique shapes that made ideal floral arrangements during winter when everything else seemed dead. I wanted to dig up seedlings to take with me, but the length of their root systems provided a challenge. Each tiny seedling only several inches high had roots a foot or more long. I persisted, digging deeper and deeper, and transplanted several in our new yard. Those little plants grew extremely large and every year they needed pruning. I never forgot how long those roots were when the seedlings were so tiny.

As I looked at the large oak, I felt the Lord speak to my heart about the oak and firethorn roots, and He said that the fruit in my life was also growing. He saw what I could not. I felt His love comfort my heart and no longer felt lonely or barren.

Through the years of my faith walk, I learned to place the Lord and His word before problems that tried to beset me. I often felt like Tamar in the early years—when neighbors excluded our fatherless home from community gatherings. Though I tried to explain to my boys that we were not invited, I salved their rejection and mine with a run to Dairy Queen.

When needed, the Lord reminds me to go back to the Word in Isaiah 54:4–5. Though I still identified with the shame and rejection of Tamar, I have learned to put on a garment of praise for the spirit of heaviness. I praised the Lord as my precious Heavenly Husband who is always with me. He has met me in marvelous ways in raising my sons, and there are now four grandchildren growing up learning to follow the Lord. Nothing is impossible with Him. He tells us in Hebrews 13:5 that He will never leave us nor forsake us. I can therefore put on that garment of praise (Isaiah 61:3); whenever I feel the spirit of heaviness trying to overtake me.

My heart's cry is for all "Tamars" to realize that nothing you ever did, and nothing done to shame or hurt you, can separate you from the love of God (Romans 8:39). The One who created you loves you. So let's put on our new garment of praise. We are no longer like Tamar—we are part of His beloved bride wearing His beautiful garment of praise.

Father God, I pray when the enemy of our souls tries to come in with our former grief and shame that You will remind us of Your beautiful garment of praise. When we praise You, shame must flee from us. I give you thanks and praise, in the Mighty Name of Jesus. Amen.

What If... I Had Never Been Sexually Abused?

Stephanie L. Jones

Trust in the LORD with all your heart and lean not on your own understanding.

PROVERBS 3:5 NIV

Let me be the first to admit that I've spent a lot of time asking what-if questions. What if I hadn't gone to that place on that day? What if I had taken that job? What if I hadn't called him back? What if? Despite knowing that pondering such questions can be a waste of time, there is one what-if question that remains at the forefront of my mind and shapes and molds my life as I know it today. What if I had never been sexually abused?

Child sexual abuse, more commonly referred to as child molestation, involves using a child for sexual purposes. Some examples of child sexual abuse include fondling, inviting a child to touch or be touched sexually, intercourse, rape, incest, and involving a child in prostitution or pornography, most of which I've experienced. According to the organization Darkness to Light, only 10 percent of sexual abuse offenses occur at the hands of a stranger. That means that 90 percent of child sexual abuse cases occur at the hands of a family member, close family friend, or trusted leader, such as a pastor or teacher. Ninety percent! Selah (pause and think about that).

My abusers were among the other 90 percent. I was taken advantage of and violated in the worst type of way by the very people I loved and trusted. Notice that I said *people* and not *person*. This was not a one-time or one-person incident for me. Several different people sexually abused me for many years. So much so that even still today, I don't think that I recall everything and possibly not everyone.

The many years of sexual abuse that I experienced as a child played a major role in the decisions that I made as a teenager and young adult. Like research has proven is the case with many sexual abuse victims, I too was sexually promiscuous, involved with older men as a young girl, and became an alcohol and substance abuser early in life. I also suffered from an identity crisis. I didn't know where I was going or who I was. I had accepted and taken on the role of being a victimized, confused, and abused young woman.

Despite these personal issues and the lifestyle that I was living, my life appeared perfect to everyone on the outside, but in reality it was anything but perfect. Watching me was like viewing a mirage of sky-blue water in the hot Arizona desert. It looked real but it just wasn't so. I covered up my pain and shame with a beaming smile, corporate ID, expensive car, and impressive wardrobe. I was too ashamed to let the real Stephanie be seen.

However, many years went by before I even realized that there was something wrong with me. I knew that I wasn't happy, but I viewed my chaotic life as normal. I thought what I'd gone through and how I felt about it was just another part of life. I'd been told that life had its ups and downs and we all had to go through something. It wasn't until the pain and shame began to spill over into my marriage that I began to see that what I was feeling inside and experiencing daily was not normal. The anxiety and panic attacks, the binge and stress eating, as well as the depression and sadness were not in God's plan for my life. Frustrated, overweight, maxed out in credit card debt, and struggling to be my husband's helpmeet, I finally sought the Lord for help.

"Lord," I cried out. "How did I get here?"

I've been told to every question there's an answer. God surely had an answer for me. It wasn't what I thought it would be, but it was my answer. He began to march me right through my past, showing me how the sexual abuse affected my life from one year to the next, especially when it came to past relationships and what I thought about sex. How could someone tell me not to have sex as a teenager? It was all that I knew. I had been taught to please a man since I was five years old.

Gradually, with God leading the way, I began to face what happened to me as a child. I started to talk openly about it, as well as release years of built-up anger. I discovered that I was angrier about the effects of the sexual abuse than I was about the act itself. That helped me to move past all of those what-if questions. I learned to accept that the abuse did happen and I couldn't get back the time that I spent living recklessly because of it. Most important, I've been able to wholeheartedly forgive those who offended me.

It has not always been easy traveling along this healing journey with God. There have been many tearful days and nights. In order to break free from the bondage of the past, I've had to stir up memories that were not pleasant to think about. But it has been worth it! While there were many instances where I simply made bad choices in life, He has shown me that what happened to me, and the repercussions from it, was not my fault. It was not my fault! Therefore, I am now free to move forward and I know that I have nothing to be ashamed of. He has healed me of the pain and taken away the shame—forever.

What if I had never been sexually abused? Like all others, there's an answer to this question too. In the past I tried to answer it on my own instead of allowing God to do it for me. Maybe I wouldn't have gotten involved in that abusive relationship. Maybe I would have graduated from college. Maybe I would have had different friends and made different choices. These were my answers. But these were not God's answers.

He began to take me through His Word, showing me how many people in both the old and new testaments had to overcome traumatic situations, some of which were the result of things done to them by the people they loved and trusted. Even Jesus was hurt by the people He loved. Yet He forgave them and moved on. Instead of allowing it to destroy Him and accepting a life of victimization and confusion, He turned it around for good. His suffering became part of His life's ministry. The abuse that He suffered is why I have the joy and freedom that I do today. So

I've decided to be like Jesus and make the abuse a part of my life's ministry!

Without the sexual abuse, I wouldn't have this redemptive story to show God's glory and mercy in my life. Without the sexual abuse I wouldn't have the ministry that I have today, traveling the world helping others get to know God's love and healing power. Without the sexual abuse, the men and women whom I have been able to help find peace and healing may have never sought help. What if I had never been sexually abused?

Father God, thank You for hearing all our questions and giving each the same answer—Jesus Christ. Though the enemy sought to do us harm, may everything in our lives be used for Your glory to win people into the kingdom. In Jesus's name, amen.

The Day of Salvation

Marilynn Griffith

*Behold, now is the accepted time;
behold, now is the day of salvation.*

2 Corinthians 6:2 KJV

A few years ago, I got an e-mail from Stanice Anderson, one of the sistahs in this book. In the message, Stanice shared her testimony of accepting Christ and urged her readers—meaning me—to share our testimonies, stories of the moment we first believed, with at least three people.

I thought about this for quite a while, about how to condense my testimony into one moment, an instant where I came face-to-face with Jesus. Which time to pick? Was it the day my knees knocked until I ran down the aisle of Canaan Missionary Baptist Church? That night under the cross at St. Joseph's Infant and Maternity Home? Perhaps it was at one of my heartfelt baptisms or anguished abortion clinic prayers?

Jesus was in all those places, from when I lost my markers in fourth grade and prayed to God to find them. He could help me, I knew. And so I followed the voice from Sunday school, the voice that whispered on the air and guided my little feet back to the playground, through the bushes . . .

"Where are you going?" the other kids said.

"Following Jesus," I shouted, winding through the sandbox and around the fence.

I'm still doing that, walking in circles, just trying to follow Jesus. And people are still poking my back asking me where I'm going. Trouble is, sometimes I don't have a clue. All I know is that he kept knocking, kept loving, until one day, out of gas, bereft of excuses and just plain tired, I fell into His lap and stayed.

And thank heaven I did. It's such a beautiful, wondrous place, the embrace of God. It's worth the search, worth the wanting. It's worth it all.

So when did I meet Jesus?

Then.

There.

Here.

Now.

Today is the day of my salvation. It's the day of yours too. Today and every day we must come to Him, call to Him, follow Him. Sometimes we fall and get broken and bruised, but just like He did with me that day on the playground, Christ takes our hands, strokes our hair, and whispers, "Follow Me."

Even if you don't know the moment or the hour when you believed, I encourage you to share with others what God has done in your life. Never underestimate the power of the blood of Jesus . . . or your testimony.

If you do not know Jesus for yourself, please pause a moment and accept our invitation into the sistahood of Christ. If you've made it this far, surely you've heard Him knocking. Close your eyes and ask Him to come in. Give Him all your stuff, even the bad things. He can handle it. We're praying for you and looking forward to hearing your story. Stop by Sistahfaith.com anytime.

Father we thank you that we overcome the enemy by the blood of the Lamb and by the word of our testimony. Help us not to love our lives so much that we shrink back from speaking what You have done in our lives. In Jesus's name, amen.

Twelve Weeks of Truth —Week Eleven

All glorious is the princess within her chamber;
her gown is interwoven with gold.
In embroidered garments she is led to the king;
her virgin companions follow her and are brought to you.
They are led in with joy and gladness;
they enter the palace of the king.

PSALM 45:13–15 NIV

DISCUSSION QUESTIONS

1. Though we showed you our scars, now we are moving full circle, back to the beginning, back to Christ. Even as we share our testimonies, we always want to end up where we began—with Jesus. Where do you feel you are in your healing process? Are you still covering or is your hurt getting air?

2. Consider silk, suede, satin, and sequins. Which is more like the "fabric" of your life right now? What kinds of things are made from this fabric? Share and discuss this.

3. How often do you laugh? Take part of your Circle time to just laugh at something, maybe at yourselves. Share what makes you laugh.

Father God, thank You for adorning me in the garment of praise. It's a perfect fit. In Jesus's name, amen.

CHAPTER TWELVE

A HEALING SEASON

When Jesus saw him lie, and knew that he had been now a long time in that case, he saith unto him, Wilt thou be made whole?

JOHN 5:6 KJV

Over the course of this book, you've gotten to know Tamar, a sistah from the Word, and many sistahs from the world. Unfortunately, Tamar stayed shut up in her brother's house and never made it to her father's house, the palace she'd left one fateful morning to show kindness to someone. The women who've lifted their skirts here and shown you their scars did so not to show their wounds, but to reveal their healing.

Have we been hurt? Yes. Have we been healed? Yes! Though there are times when our memories itch and stir, we have come to accept ourselves, forgive others, and trust God. By allowing air to get to our wounds along with the healing water of God's word, something happened to us that we never thought possible: the pain we once felt turned into passion and that passion turned into purpose.

Look through the biographies at the end of this book and you will not find victims, you'll find victorious women of God! So lift up your head, sistah. Let go of your hurt: your anger, bitterness, and blame. Stay safe and use wisdom in the earthly world, but in the spirit, get free. Reclaim your wings and your words, your gifts and your glory.

Reach out to Christ and accept His cup of living water, His offer to make you whole. He's more than able. We'll be here too, the women of this book, just beyond the walls of you, arms outstretched and words open wide. Go wild enough to believe all the way beyond shame.

Take time out and come away with Christ to enter a new season. A healing season. And don't forget to bring somebody with you.

Raising the Roof

Marilynn Griffith

And many were gathered together, so that there was no longer room, not even near the door; and He was speaking the word to them. And they came, bringing to Him a paralytic, carried by four men. Being unable to get to Him because of the crowd, they removed the roof above Him; and when they had dug an opening, they let down the pallet on which the paralytic was lying.

MARK 2:2–4 NASB

When New York Representative Shirley Chisholm died, she said she wanted to be remembered as having guts. That's exactly how I remember her. From her big, fluffy hair to her words, tinged with the curried speech of Barbados, I remember being proud of her and thinking she was the type of person who'd dig a hole in the roof and lower you down to where you could get some help. And she wouldn't drop you either, but put the cot through the ceiling easy-like. Steady.

I have women in my life like that, roof raisers who claw through mud and rock to get me to Jesus, who pray heaven and earth slap together for me in those times when I'm stuck and can't move. My mother does that for me too, has always done it since back in the day when she ran me down on Sunday mornings and dragged me out of folks' houses with a fresh pair of pantyhose in one hand and her Bible in the other. Now, sometimes, I dig through the house and lower her down too, though not always as gently as I'd like.

Sistah stories do that for me too. They make me see a rigid part of my life and while I listen to the words, turn the pages, my heart goes deeper, until I hear the voice of the Savior and feel the crumbled plaster in my hair. I want to do that for people, both in my life and in my writing. I want you to do it too.

So the next time you find a woman still lying where you left her, stiff and unmoving, don't ignore her. Don't try to force her limbs into place. Just nod to some friends to get the other corners and lift her onto your backs.

And bring a spoon either for digging through or celebrating after. Sometimes, roofs are thicker than they look.

Father God, I need sistahs around me, people to support me. And I need to learn how I can be a better roof raiser myself. Teach me how to do that, and lead me to others who will do that for me. In Jesus's name, amen.

Brother, I'm Healed

Marilynn Griffith

I see you there, smiling
With that gap-toothed grin
Since you wink, you don't think
I remember back then.

I know all about it,
Her stolen best things,
The pearls and the rubies,
Crushed hopes, lost rings.

They said she hollered,
But you wouldn't hear,
You couldn't be bothered
To silence her fear.

She kept on screaming,
Until Forever heard,
He tasted her dreaming,
Held her soft, like a bird.

You think I don't know you,
As you squint at my hair,
At the back of your eyes,
I see the truth there.

She told me all about it,
The mess that was you,
He made her shout it,
All the black and the blue.

She let you go then
Like I'm 'bout to now,

Lips bright with hope
Too much truth on my brow

Fists clenched, at a loss
You fear it is me
You finger a cross,
Too tangled to free.

You try to speak,
But I shake my head,
I'm not who you seek,
The girl from that bed.

You drop to your knees,
Reach out with your hand,
Begging me please,
Like I don't understand.

He calls to you,
Bent over and kneeled,
I keep standing true,
Saying, "Brother, I'm healed."

A Bare Witness

Marilynn Griffith

We are not trying to please men but God, who tests our hearts. You know we never used flattery, nor did we put on a mask to cover up greed—God is our witness. We were not looking for praise from men, not from you or anyone else.

1 THESSALONIANS 2:4–6 NIV

My second son's birthday is also mine in a way, though it doesn't mark the beginning of my life, but the start of a journey with God.

For me, it is a birthday of the soul.

It was around the time of his birth God began to shake me, to rattle my bones. The skeletons in my closet, even. During that time, God provided me a space in which to be comforted in my affliction. And afflicted I was. The Jesus breeze during those days was sweet. Satisfying. For the first time in years, my clenched fists opened and my hands fell at my sides, palms up, ready to receive. And there was so much to receive. Day by day, I feasted on God's word, sometimes stumbling, always wanting . . . Him.

Unfortunately, as time went on, my comfort became comfortable and though it's easy on the mind, such a state rots the soul. And so came the wind, the shaking of my little Jesus tree house, built so sturdy on my own expectations, my interpretations of this cut-and-dried wrong-or-right God, so bright with no darkness at all. Thunder rumbled in my ears as my tree bent low. The Son seemed to leave the sky, leaving a gray, mysterious fog behind.

I recognized that fog. Once it had clouded all of God from me. Now it only shadowed the outlines of Him, allowing me to see the pale shadow of my own making, cut and pasted from word-pictures painted by men. To see even the hand of this God, this Jesus, I would have to get up.

I'd have to move.

I'd have to bleed.

I would have to shatter the mask, once a filter from the world and now a smothering menace, so tightly grafted to my face.

It took time to peel it off. Day by day, I peeled and scraped through the layers so painstakingly applied. He brought women to help me, truth to chisel away the painted smile, courage to scrape the fake Jesus speech from my tongue. Trials came to rip at my robe of self-righteousness, leaving me uncovered.

Or so I thought.

"We can begin now. But don't paint your heart again, no matter how tempting. Regardless of where I take you, stay sheer so I can see you. Remain a bare witness," I heard in my heart when I least expected it.

The direction sounded simple, but it isn't easy. I don't always succeed. My heart often wants something thick to robe it, a pelt of pride to keep out the cold. Even the heaviness of shame can be tempting, threatening to curl around me in soft deception. It is then that the life-quakes come, whisking it away from my shoulders.

In the eyes of pretty women on padded pews I see the same struggles. Women who don't dare to lift their masks an inch, not even for a breath, lest they lose their placement on the ladder to nowhere. I smile at them, these women who don't want to hear about the other me. Women who've forgotten the other them. Women who don't dare comfort certain people because to do so, they'd have to . . . tell.

And so, telling is the task my friends and I are given. Though the names and places are different, the story is always the same. Love came, when we least expected it, when we most needed it.

So we walk the floors and tell the tales. Afterward, when someone grabs my arm and digs in her nails, staring at me with that knowing look, I watch and pray as the first of the heart paint washes away, knowing that though she thinks this is the end, it is only the beginning.

You can't go naked with everybody. I get that. Going bare without God's call or covering can be more trouble than help. Hiding away forever, though, isn't an option. We have to find someone, someplace, to be real, to tell about a girl we once knew . . . who became new.

We are His beloved. And He is ours. Take off your shame and see yourself as God does—accepted, redeemed, and loved.

A bare witness.

Father God, I long to be real, vulnerable, bare before You and my sistahs. Help me to find the courage to do so. Help me find women I can trust. Protect me, even as I take off my armor. In Jesus's name, amen.

HEALING PROCLAMATION PRAYERS

(To be spoken aloud—in front of a mirror, if possible.)

Forgiving Fathers

Father God, I thank You that I am no longer the walking wounded but the healed hopeful. Though earthly fathers may fail, You never fail. I accept my father for who he was and who he is, knowing that it is my Father in heaven who defines who I am. In Jesus's name, amen.

Forgiving Mothers

Father God, I thank You for my mother. I release and forgive her for any times that I felt she hurt me or failed to protect me. I accept her for who she is, as she is, knowing that You did the same for me. In Jesus's name, amen.

Forgiving Male Abusers

Lord, I forgive every man who has hurt me mentally, physically, emotionally, or sexually. I release them so that I can take hold of Your blessings with both hands. As You heal my brokenness, heal theirs as well. In Jesus's name, amen.

Forgiving Female Abusers

Lord, I forgive every woman who has hurt me mentally, physically, emotionally, or sexually. I release them so that I can take hold of Your blessings with both hands. As You heal my brokenness, heal theirs as well. In Jesus's name, amen.

Blessing the Brothers

Bless the good men in the lives of myself and my sistahs, Lord—husbands, fathers, brothers, relatives, and friends—princes You sent to cherish and love Your daughters in ways we didn't know were possible. Help us get whole enough to accept their love and return it in a way that is pleasing to You and reflects the worth You've assigned to us. In Jesus's name, amen.

Salvation Prayer

I accept Jesus Christ as the lover of my soul and the Lord of my life. I gratefully accept that He died for my sins. I open the door of my heart to Him and say, "Yes, I will be made whole. I am willing and wanting to be healed. And once I am healed, show me how to bring others out of darkness!" In Jesus's name, amen.

Body Blessing

I bless myself now, from head to toe. I hug myself, holding my body and declaring it beautiful. May every step I take from here leave blessings behind me. I pull up the root of bitterness and ask to be rooted and grounded in Your love. Reveal any unforgiveness in me and heal anything in my body that has resulted from it. In Jesus's name, amen.

Sistahood Prayer

Thank you for sending sistahs to hold me with their words and remind me that the most important thing about scars isn't the wound, but the healing! Help me to use my gifts and words to be Your healing hands. In Jesus's name, amen.

Bible Sistah Prayer

Thank you for Tamar, Lord, and for using her to remind me that evil is nothing new. I pray that I've learned something about being a woman, a Christian, and a friend in these pages. Give me the courage to get real with the safe women in my life, to have ears to hear and words to tell my own stories. In Jesus's name, amen.

Gentle Spirit Prayer

Help me to speak gently to my mother, sisters, coworkers, and friends, even when they talk to me crazy. Help me remember that shame can bring a sistah down. Use my hands to lift someone up. In Jesus's name, amen.

Guidance Prayer

Grow me, Lord. Know me, Lord. Show me where to walk. May nothing I do in word or deed diminish the price You paid for me: the blood of Your own Son. Put my feet on pleasant paths. In the name of the One who keeps us from falling, Jesus Christ, amen.

Twelve Weeks of Truth —Week Twelve

A time to tear and a time to mend . . .

ECCLESIASTES 3:7 NIV

DISCUSSION QUESTIONS

1. This book is a great start on your healing journey. Each day, go to God and ask Him to heal your heart and fill your hands with love and laughter. Write a special prayer for someone in the group who has been a blessing to you and bring it to the SistahFaith Circle meeting.

2. There is a time to tear and a time to mend. Make room in your life for healing. If you are already in a good place, make room—with boundaries, of course—in your life for listening. Complete your testimony and present a five-minute version to share with the group.

3. Tamar never made it to her father's house, but we have Jesus to help lead us home. Pray for the women who you know might benefit from this book and give them a copy. Pray for the sistahs in your circle. Commit to keeping in touch and get together at least once a month to do something fun. Get everyone's contact information before you leave (if you don't have it already).

Father God, we thank You for this time we've spent getting to know You—and one another—better. We thank You for Tamar and the reminder that You can take away our heaviness of heart and clothe us in Your praise. Help us to do Your will on the earth. In Jesus's name, amen.

HEALING RESOURCES

Recovery Resources

Rape Abuse and Incest National Network (RAINN), National Sexual Assault Online Hotline: www.rainn.org, 1-800-656-HOPE

National Domestic Violence Hotline: www.ndvh.org, 1-800-799-SAFE (7233) or 1-800-787-3224

National Teen Dating Abuse Hotline: www.loveisrespect.org, 1-866-331-9474 or 1-866-331-8453

Project Rachel: www.hopeafterabortion.com, 1-800-5WE-CARE

Other Resources

www.ilovetolisten.com (hearing the stories of others)
www.freedomintruth.org

Books

Victory over the Darkness: Realizing the Power of Your Identity in Christ, by Neil T. Anderson

Victory over the Darkness: Realizing the Power of Your Identity in Christ Study Guide, by Neil T. Anderson

The Wounded Heart: Hope for Adult Victims of Childhood Sexual Abuse, by Dan B. Allender

The Bondage Breaker: Overcoming Negative Thoughts, Irrational Feelings, Habitual Sins, by Neil T. Anderson

Boundaries: When to Say Yes, When to Say No to Take Control of Your Life, by Henry Cloud and John Townsend

Boundaries with Kids, by Henry Cloud and John Townsend

The Lies We Tell Ourselves, by Dr. Chris Thurman

Tilly, by Frank E. Peretti

ABOUT THE CONTRIBUTORS

STANICE ANDERSON: Sistah Stanice is an author, speaker, and playwright. She has appeared on *The 700 Club*, NPR, ABC News Radio, and many other shows. Her *Sistahfaith* stories were excerpted from her book, *I Say a Prayer for Me: One Woman's Life of Faith and Triumph*. Formerly employed at usatoday.com, Stanice is a freelance writer for many magazines as well as her own inspirational e-mail series, Food for the Spirit. To hear her weekly podcast, Faith-Lift, visit www.myspace.com/isayaprayerforme.

TANYA R. BATES: Tanya R. Bates is a native of Rockford, Illinois, and a graduate of Fisk University. Her vision is to create works of art that inspire, motivate, and encourage women of all ages. Her interests include: singing, playing the piano, writing, reading, spending time with family, art, and more. She currently resides in Lansing, Michigan, with her husband. Tanya is the author of *One Day's Peace: A Woman's Journey Through Life*.

CLAUDIA MAIR BURNEY: Claudia Mair Burney is the author of the popular Ragamuffin Diva blog and the novel *Zora and Nicky: A Novel in Black and White*. She is also the author of the Amanda Bell Brown mysteries and the Exorsistah series for teens. Her work has appeared in *Discipleship Journal* magazine, *The One Year Life Verse Devotional*, and *Justice in the Burbs*. She lives in Michigan with her husband, five of their seven children, and a quirky dwarf rabbit. She loves hearing from readers at claudia .mair.burney@gmail.com.

WANDA J. BURNSIDE: Sistah Wanda is an award-winning poet and writer with over five-hundred poems, twenty-two performed plays, and eight gospel plays to her credit. She is president of the Called and Ready Writers of Detroit. Visit her on the web at www .thecalledandreadywriters.org/wburnside.htm.

ROBIN CALDWELL: Sistah Robin is the founder and CEO of J Standard Publicity LLC. When she's not being a conduit of blessings or helping writers birth their books, she can be found in Starbucks sipping a little latte and making big moves. If you look real close, between the commas of this book, you might make out her fingerprints. Visit Robin on the web at www.thejstandard .com.

SHELETTE CARLISLE: Sistah Shelette is a poet, mother, and lover of God. She lives with her family in Florida. Contact her at info@sistahfaith.com.

LADY CATHERINE: Sistah Lady Catherine is a writer of all sorts and a minister of the gospel, teaching on family and the personal gifts our Lord has given us. She has traveled to many nations to share the "good news" with all people. She resides in Florida with her darling, godly husband and two sons. You can send her an e-mail at info@sistahfaith.com.

ETTERLENE "BUNNY" DEBARGE: Best known for her years in the singing group Debarge and being the oldest of her nine talented siblings, Sistah Bunny is also a testimony to God's restoring power. Happily married with four children, Bunny chronicles how God has kept her family through both good times and bad in her book, *The Kept Ones*.

DEE EAST: Suddenly widowed after nearly ten years of marriage with three small sons, Sistah Dee spent the first six years in shock and grief. A revelation of Jesus profoundly changed her family. Dee's experience gave her a desire to help other widows. She now leads a group called the Widow's Might that gathers for

Bible study, prayer, and sharing. It is Dee's joy to see empty lives realize their importance to God and His Body. Contact Dee at deast918@comcast.net.

SHARON EWELL FOSTER: Sistah Sharon is an acclaimed author, speaker, and teacher. She has contributed to *Daily Guideposts,* Tavis Smiley's *Keeping the Faith,* and to the *Women of Color Devotional Bible.* Her achievements include the Christy Award, the Gold Pen Award, the *Romantic Times* award for Best Inspirational Novel, *Publishers Weekly* starred reviews, and the *Essence* bestseller list. Sharon also ghostwrote a *New York Times* bestselling novel. Visit her on the web at www.sharonewellfoster .com.

DORIEN HAGE: Despite being an underemployed single mom, Sistah Dorien obtained a professional certification after seven years of trying. She is currently working the job of her dreams. She recently became a finalist for a prestigious writing award. You can send her e-mail at info@sistahfaith.com.

DR. GAIL M. HAYES: Sistah Gail is founder and CEO of Daughters of the King Ministries. She is the author of several books, including *Daughters of the King: Finding Victory Through Your God-Given Personal Style.* A popular speaker, Gail helps women and businesspeople step into their destiny by discovering their identity and grasping their purpose. To invite Dr. Gail to speak to your group or just say hello, contact her at info@ daughtersoftheking.org.

DR. NAIMA JOHNSTON: Sistah Naima is a singer, speaker, educator, and founder and CEO of Broken Box Ministries, a Christian entertainment and education company. Blessed to open for gospel great Dorinda Clark Cole as well as record her own CD, Naima lives in Fairborn, Ohio, with her beloved Chihuahua Bianca, who is not spoiled but abundantly blessed! To learn more about Dr. Johnston, visit her at www.shoutlife.com/Naima.

DELORES M. JONES, MSW, LMSW: Sistah Delores is a social worker, radio host and producer, professor, dancer, and a testimony for women everywhere. Rising out of a childhood of homelessness and candlelit homework, she emerged as an award-winning journalist. She has shared her story on *The Oprah Winfrey Show* and was included in the book *Come on, People: On the Path from Victims to Victors,* by Dr. Bill Cosby and Dr. Alvin Poussaint. She has also been a news anchor on *The Tom Joyner Morning Show* and host to several shows for women on National Public Radio. When she's not mentoring women, Delores spends time roller skating, leading worship, and proclaiming the works of God. Visit her at www.deloresinspiresme.com.

STEPHANIE JONES: Sistah Stephanie is an author, speaker, and advocate for victims of childhood sexual abuse. In her book, *The Enemy Between My Legs*, she shares her own story in an open and honest way. Stephanie continues to speak with victims, especially teens and young adults, making her a sought-after speaker for schools, churches, and other organizations. She lives in the metro Detroit area with her husband. Visit her on the web at www .stephanieljones.com.

CARMITA MCCALL: In addition serving as president and CEO of Brightside International, a video, music production, and graphic design firm, Sistah Carmita mentors young writers. She is also an accomplished speaker and recording artist and the author of *My Soul Took Flight: The Poetic Journal.* Visit her online at www .carmitaonline.com.

LAVONN NEIL: Sistah LaVonn is a sought-after speaker on personal development, entrepreneurship, women, and youth issues. She is founder and CEO of Reflections, a nonprofit organization assisting victims of sexual and domestic abuse. Visit her on the web at www.unveilingthemask.com.

CARLEAN SMITH: Sistah Carlean is a native of Detroit, Michigan, where she started a ministry for women from abusive pasts called Women for Christ, a ministry dedicated to restoring women to wholeness in Christ after emotional, physical, sexual, and drug abuse. Carlean has one son, three grandchildren, and lots of laughter and love. She now lives and works in Daytona Beach, Florida. She is working on her first novel. Visit Carlean at her blog: fearlessreflection.blogspot.com.

DAVIDAE "DEE" STEWART: Sistah Dee is an editor, book reviewer, and speaker. Her works have appeared in *Mosaic Literary Magazine, Gospel Today, Romantic Times, Spirit-Led Writer,* the *Soul Source, Precious Times,* and *Rejoice!* She resides in Georgia with her daughter and family. Check her out on the web at www.christianfiction.blogspot.com.

SONYA VISOR: Sistah Sonya is a co-pastor, author, speaker, and playwright. She lives in Racine, Wisconsin, with her pastor husband and two sons. Sonya's calling is to reach out to women who are broken, knowing that God is the only one who made her whole. Visit Sonya at www.sonyavisor.com.

LITTLE SALLY WALKER: Sistah Saundra is a freelance writer living in the Dallas metropolitan area. She leads a quiet, simple life and spends most of her time reading and writing. She has authored several short stories, articles, and poems. She is currently in the process of creating her first novel. In addition to writing, Saundra enjoys gardening, decorating, and crocheting.

ROSALYN "ROS" WEBB: Sistah Rosalyn T. Webb is a freelance videographer, graphic designer, and cofounder of Brightside Media. When not doing cutting-edge media productions, Rosalyn serves on advisory boards for several Florida community organizations for women and youth. Rosalyn is also the author of the poetry book, *To Whom It May Concern.* Visit her on the web at www.justros.com.

ROBIN R. WISE: Sistah Robin is a playwright, grandmother, Sunday school teacher, and seeker of God's presence. Death to take her life from a young age, but God had another plan. Growing up, she had a secret place where she would run to pray, write, and bask in God's presence. Today, she is discovering places God has for her as well and taking her son's advice to laugh when she can. When she's not interceding or working with youth, she dreams of opening a travel agency where people can enjoy God's blessings. Though her heart goes around the world, Robin resides in Arkansas.

KISHA WOODS: Sistah Kisha grew up in Southern California, the daughter of an evangelist mother and alcoholic father. She had seven siblings but often felt alone. After an abusive relationship, God began to restore Kisha's heart, even bringing her a fantastic husband to share her life with. She lives with her husband and children and praises God daily for restoring her dignity and her life.

About the Editor/Compiler

MARILYNN GRIFFITH: Sistah Marilynn is wife to a deacon, mom to a tribe, and proof that God gives second chances. When she's not driving her kids around or serving at church, she writes novels about faith and forgiveness and speaks to women and writers about reaching their dreams. Visit her website at www .marilynngriffith.com.

For more information about starting a SistahFaith Circle or joining SistahFaith, Inc., please visit www.sistahfaith.com.

Reading Group Guide

INTRODUCTION

In this personal and powerful nonfiction collection, Marilynn Griffith brings together stories that reflect both the pain and healing of abuse. Along with these stories, we also learn the story of Tamar, King David's daughter who was raped by her half-brother in 2 Kings 13. The book is also about sisterhood and the desire for friendships that are honest but hopeful. The study guides included in each chapter can help readers form SistahFaith circles in their churches, book clubs, and neighborhoods.

Among the notable contributors are Bunny DeBarge, who details her own story of tragedy and triumph. Other highlights include: "The Naked Lady in the Yard" and "I Loved a Boy" by Claudia Mair Burney, "Treasure in the Scars" by award-winning historical novelist Sharon Ewell Foster, "Amazed by Grace" by Stanice Anderson, and "Going Home" by Dorien Hage.

The use of both poetry and prose gives the book a good rhythm for women and their friends to come together for a time of emotional and spiritual healing. Each story offers an entry into the reality and humanity of sisters of faith.

Layered with opportunities for discovery and recovery, *SistahFaith* faces the invisible visitor in many churches and women's group—shame—head-on, joining the lives of modern-day women with Tamar from the Bible. Whether a woman has experienced abuse or not, this book is one that every mother, friend, or sister should read.

QUESTIONS AND TOPICS
FOR DISCUSSION

1. This book was born out of discussions and writing between Marilynn and her friends. Did you feel a connectedness or kinship between any of the writers? Why do you think friendship is so important to women? Are you in search of sistahood?

2. Marilynn talks about finally being able to empathize with her mother's pain after experiencing her own. Have you ever been able to comfort someone because you share their experience? Was there ever a point in your life when you started to better understand what your mother has been through?

3. One theme in the collection is taking off our masks and being true to ourselves. Which story or stories do you feel expressed this theme?

4. In "I Loved a Boy," Claudia Mair Burney writes, "He was an amazing boy. Bright and warm like the sun, and just as beautiful. I remember the first time I saw him. I thought to myself, 'He's out of my league. What could he possibly see in me?' Let me tell you, if it starts with you feeling unworthy of him . . . it's gonna end badly." Have you ever gone into a relationship feeling unworthy of another person's love or

attention? How did it end? After reading this story, what were your reflections on your own first sexual experience?

5. Though most of the perpetrators of violence in the volume happen to be men, there are women. In "Confession is Good for the Soul," Stanice Anderson tells how a friend left her in an apartment full of men to be raped. Which other stories show the role that women played in violence against other women?

6. At the end of the book, there is a poem called, "Brother, I'm Healed," describing a woman who meets a man who once hurt her on the street. This time, he is afraid, afraid that she will expose what others already see. Have you ever been hurt by someone and later had to face them? How did you react? After reading this book, would you react differently?

7. After experiencing abuse, some women struggle with alcohol and drug abuse. Read "Winter is Past" by Carlean Smith. How did the event that happened when she was seventeen affect her? For how long? What hope could you share with another woman trying to stay clean and sober from this and other stories in the book?

8. Discuss the book's structure. Though there are Bible passages and prayers, this isn't your average Bible study. Were you more able to relate to the book with candid personal

stories, or did it take you some time to get used to the structure? Having read the book, would you like to read another book in this format?

9. How did you feel about the story of Tamar? Have you read it previously? Why do you think that the author gave the image of being clothed in the garments of praise? Was this a comforting concept?

10. Sexual abuse and domestic violence against women continues to climb, especially among girls. High school girlfriends are now hiding the battering that was once reserved for their mothers. How do you think we can empower girls so that they don't get into abusive relationships? How can this book be used as a tool to help girls see their worth?

11. The author referred to the compilation of stories as the act of "lifting our skirts to show our scars." This, too, is a powerful image. Do you think that there are scars under the skirts of the church when it comes to sexual abuse and domestic violence against women? How can churches and clergy reach out to hurting women in their congregations in a way that is safe and helpful for all involved?

12. Often people think of those who have been abused as victims or weaklings who should have been stronger. Did reading the stories of the smart, strong, and faithful women in this book make you think about abuse differently? Can you

see how everyone—including the perpetrators—gets hurt in these situations? In what ways has this book changed your opinion about victims of violence?

13. Do you see any common threads in the stories that were included? What story affected you most? Who would you most like to share that story with? What exercises and strategies can you take from this book to deal with difficult people and situations?

Use these final pages to tell the truth about your own pain. Whether you share your story with someone else or simply leave it enclosed in the pages of this book, just the telling will bring you a measure of triumph.

_____

_____

_____

_____

_____

_____

_____

_____

_____

_____

_____

_____

_____

_____

_____

_____

_____